MW00573071

THE TECI
OF ASTRAL PROJECTION

In this densely documented study, Dr Crookall
examines the practical methods of inducing astral
projection, explaining techniques for releasing the
astral body and providing a wealth of detail relating to
every aspect of astral travel.

THE TECHNIQUES
OF ASTRAL PROJECTION

Denouement after fifty years

by

ROBERT CROOKALL

B.Sc. (Psychology), D.Sc., Ph.D.
(Formerly Demonstrator in Botany, University of Aberdeen;
Late Principal Geologist, H.M. Geological Survey, London)
Member of the Society for Psychical Research;
Member of the Churches' Fellowship for Psychical and Spiritual Studies

THE AQUARIAN PRESS
Wellingborough, Northamptonshire

First published 1964
Sixth Impression 1977
First paperback edition February 1981
Second Impression November 1981

ISBN 0 85030 261 7

Printed in Great Britain by
King's English Bookprinters Limited, Bramley, Leeds,
and bound by Weatherby Woolnough,
Wellingborough, Northamptonshire.

CONTENTS

"He that answereth a matter before he heareth it, it is a shame and a folly unto him."—*Solomon.*

"He that gives reason for what he saith has done what is fit to be done and the most that can be done. He that gives no reason speaks nothing, though he saith never so much."—*Benjamin Whichcote.*

"The ancient idea that man is a microcosm, or little world in himself, developing in response to the Macrocosm, or Universe, and having its counterpart in his own being, is a far more adequate conception than the prevailing attempt to envisage man as an evolving animal."—*Dr J. Parton Milum.*

"It is evident that, when many coincide in their testimony (where no previous concert can have taken place), the probability resulting from this concurrence does not rest on the supposed veracity of each considered separately, but on the improbability of such agreement taking place by chance. For, though in such a case the witnesses should be considered as unworthy of credit, ... still the chances would be *infinite* against their all agreeing in the same falsehood."—*Archbishop Richard Whately.*

"A mind unwilling to believe ... will insist on taking that evidence to bits and rejecting them item by item. *Modern logic has made it plain that simple facts can never be 'proved' except by their coherence in a system.* But, as all facts come singly, anyone who dismisses them one by one is destroying the conditions under which the conviction of new truth could arise in his mind."—*Professor F. C. S. Schiller.*

"Faith in God should not be a substitute for scientific study, but a stimulus to it, for our intellectual faculties are God's gift to us."—*Archbishop William Temple.*

"The only road to a fuller grasp of Reality is the exploration of 'super-normal' perception."—*Dr Albert Schweitzer.*

PREFACE

LORD BYRON said, "Truth is always strange, stranger than fiction." Longfellow declared, "All things come round to him who will but wait."

In these pages we shall consider a matter that, if true, is far stranger than the fictions in our novels. It has taken half a century to bring about the dénouement.

Dr Hereward Carrington, who died two or three years ago, was one of the foremost psychical researchers in the world and the only one who (until recent years) was active in investigating astral projection (or out-of-the-body experiences). In 1920 he published a book entitled *Higher Psychical Phenomena*. In this he stated, "I epitomized everything I had been able to unearth dealing with this important subject [of astral projection]." He (op. cit., p. 284) quoted a number of techniques, or exercises, designed for the production of astral projections, and described the paper in which they had been originally given, namely, *Journal* A.S.P.R., X, 1916, pp. 632–60; 679–708, as the "excellent work" of Prescott F. Hall. In point of fact these techniques were not Hall's (who was thoroughly sceptical concerning all psychic matters), but had been received by Hall in *"communications" from supposed discarnate souls.*[1]

Hall had two friends who claimed to be able to project their Astral Bodies, or "doubles", at will. He wished to check up upon these claims by obtaining the necessary "know-how" in "communications" and try them for himself. It may be added that the medium concerned knew nothing, and cared nothing, about astral projection.

Since 1916, when these "excellent" communications were published, a number of investigators, including the present writer,

[1] Hall merely gave a "digest" of the (350 pages of) "communications", arranging the subjects mentioned in alphabetical order—and thereby confusing the situation considerably. The language employed was that of the "communicators" (op. cit., 1916, p. 640): Hyslop (op. cit., 1916, p. 632) defended this procedure, saying, "It is not amiss to use the terms more or less as they came in the records." Hall included half a dozen sentences of preliminary and incidental observations only. The "excellent work" for which Dr Carrington expressed his indebtedness to *Hall* must be credited to *"communicators"*! What was their nature? Although this can never be "scientifically proved", it may well be a matter of practical certainty.

have collected and studied the testimonies of astral projectors. It is now clear that Mrs Keeler's "communicators", whoever or whatever they were, knew a great deal more about astral projection than Hall, Carrington or (so far as we are aware) by any other living person. Such being the case, they can scarcely have been "sub-conscious" fragments of the total mind of Mrs Keeler (or of the sceptical Hall). They claimed, in fact, to be orientals and it should be noted that a number of the techniques they gave (pp. 652, 682, 690) were used centuries ago in ancient Egypt, etc.

It would seem to be difficult to avoid the conclusion that these "communicators" were indeed, as claimed, orientals who had survived bodily death. If this is admitted, then it constitutes indirect evidence for survival.

Some of our castles (e.g. that at Rochester) were apparently impregnable: they successfully resisted all direct attacks. Yet many fell to indirect approach (Rochester for lack of drains!). The problem of survival has proved almost, if not quite, impregnable to direct attack: yet matters such as those here considered, though constituting evidence of an indirect kind, leave the matter in little, if any, doubt.

R. CROOKALL

Woodland Avenue
Dursley, Glos.

INTRODUCTION

In every period of man's history some people have claimed to have had an experience that to others was pure fantasy—they claimed to have left their physical bodies in a second body (a non-physical one which they variously called the "Astral", "Etheric", "Spirit", "Spiritual", "Soul", "Four-dimensional", etc. Body) and declared that they thought, felt, saw, heard, and acted in it. These out-of-the-body experiences are popularly called astral projections on the assumption that an objective "Astral Body" was, in fact, projected from, or released by, the familiar physical body. St Paul (2 Cor. xii, 2) mentioned a case of this kind and many reputable people, including Roman Catholic Saints and Quakers, have had such experiences.

The existence of out-of-the-body experiences, then, is certain: what is in doubt is the exact nature of the "Astral Body", i.e. whether it is always a hallucination (a mental image) or whether it is sometimes a "real", objective (though non-physical) body. In some instances there was doubtless nothing whatever of an objective nature—the supposed "Astral Body" was merely imagined. But if, in other instances, an objective body was involved, the matter is of very great importance to us all.

In 1961 I cited a hundred and sixty first-hand descriptions of out-of-the-body experiences in a book entitled *The Study and Practice of Astral Projection* (Aquarian Press). In the conclusions (p. 140) I advanced reasons for concluding that many of the "Astral Bodies" there described had not been imagined but were "real" and objective. Over two hundred further cases are given in a book entitled *More Astral Projections* shortly to be published by Aquarian Press. Many point to the same conclusion. If the latter is justified, then the probability that we survive the death of the physical body is very great—the "Astral", "Etheric" or "Soul" Body would, in fact, be the mechanism of survival.

HISTORICAL DATA

In 1919 Dr Hereward Carrington published *Modern Psychical Phenomena* (Kegan Paul, Trench Trubner & Co. Ltd.) which

included a chapter (X, pp. 146–54) on this subject. After mention-
ing the work of Durville, Baraduc and de Rochas, he dealt with
that of Dr Charles Lancelin (Méthodes de Dédoublement Person-
nel) which concerned the externalization, from the physical body,
of (a) "neuricity" or nervous force (or the Astral Body in which
it is supposed to circulate) and (b) the "sensibility". Lancelin held
that, while everyone releases some small amount of "nervous
force", psychics and mediums are such because they release it in
considerable amounts. He found that the externalization was at its
maximum in psychics who were calm and serene in mind and
healthy in body.

The techniques which he advocated for the projection, or release, of the "Astral Body" were as follows:

1. Arouse and "super-charge" the "sub-conscious" will by
giving it certain verbal suggestions ("I have *will*!", "I have
energy!", etc.) just before entering sleep; continue them until
actually falling asleep.

2. *Imagine* that the Astral Body loosens from, and eventually
leaves, the physical body.

3. Transfer the consciousness from the physical body to the
released Astral Body (using it as a vehicle, or instrument, of the
Soul—for seeing, hearing, etc.).

4. Move some little distance, in the Astral Body, from the
physical body, making observations and experiments (e.g. try to
go through a wall; see whether or not you are seen by some
person, whether or not he feels your touch).

Lancelin observed that projection was facilitated by certain
conditions. On the day of the experiment, little food should be
taken or release will be difficult, if indeed possible. The atmosphere should be dry and clear, with a high barometer (not
humid and "muggy", with a low barometer). High electrical conditions, i.e. thunderstorms, etc., interfere with good results. The
temperature should be high (say 20° below body-temperature) at
the time of the experiment. The possibility of disturbances (e.g.
sudden loud noises) should be eliminated, since rapid return may
be unpleasant. The best time is between 11 p.m. and 3 a.m., i.e.
when one is most likely to fall into a natural sleep.

In 1920 Carrington published *Higher Psychical Phenomena* (Kegan
Paul, Trench Trubner & Co. Ltd.) which also included a chapter

(XIII, pp. 266–89) on these matters. He said, "The *exteriorization of 'sensitivity'* has been studied by the French; and its complement, its opposite, is *the 'exteriorization' of the motive force or 'motivity'—where the nervous energy of the body is projected* beyond the surface of the body, into space, and there moves material objects [= telekinesis], or has some effect upon the material world."

"This Astral Body, which is *the feeling body, the emotional body*, has been experimentally detached from the physical, by means of *deep magnetic passes*; and when the subject is in a 'mesmeric' trance, as distinct from the hypnotic. 'Mesmeric' and 'magnetic' phenomena are *not* the same as hypnotic.[1] Hypnotism deals entirely with the mind, and is due to 'suggestion'—mental influences; but 'magnetism' and 'mesmerism' depend upon a certain physical effluence or influence which passes from the operator to the subject—that sometimes forms a sort of vital connecting-link, establishing a *rapport* between subject and operator, in the same way that the vital energy is enabled to move a material, physical object, when that object is charged with it. One step beyond this *experimental* detachment of the Astral Body is *voluntary* projection."

Carrington added the work of Dr F. Van Eeden and the Yogis to that of de Rochas, Durville, Baraduc, Lancelin, etc. He also (pp. 278, 282) credited Prescott F. Hall, an American investigator, with certain most interesting statements concerning projection. These statements, however, were not by Hall—they were *"communications"*, including techniques for projection and the effects of applying them, that Hall had received through the mediumship of Mrs Minnie E. Keeler (see *Journal* A.S.P.R., X, 1916, pp. 632–61, 679–708).

Carrington (op. cit., 1920, p. 284) cited a number of the techniques that had been given in the *"communications"* and said, in a footnote, "I am indebted to *Mr Prescott Hall's excellent work for a number*[2] *of the exercises.*"

[1] This is not the general view.
[2] Although Carrington acknowledged only "a number" of these exercises, all that he gave (except perhaps that of imagining climbing a ladder) were given by the *"communicators"* (see *Journal* A.S.P.R., X, 1916, pp. 644, 652, 690, 694, 706 respectively) and were not *Hall's* work in any sense. The latter consisted in preparing a "digest" of the "communications" he had received. He retained the language used by the "communicators" (op. cit., pp. 632, 640). The occasional preliminary comments which Hall made (p. 650 regarding colours seen, p. 657 regarding odours smelled, and p. 682 regarding "elementals" seen constitute only half-a-dozen sentences in the forty-six pages.

It will be clear that Carrington's (quite appropriate) acknowledgement of "excellence" should have been made not to *Hall* but to the *"communicators"*! Hall's alphabetical digest is very confusing and includes much repetition.

Hall (op. cit., p. 640) tried the exercises recommended by the *"communicators"*, made a few preliminary and occasional observations in the "digest" and promised to give his complete findings in *"a later paper"*.

We hope to show that the tribute (of "excellent work") unwittingly applied by Carrington to the "communications" received through Mrs Keeler may now be extended from *the numerous techniques and exercises* provided to facilitate projection to *the numerous bodily events and mental experiences which they described as encountered in projections*.

In 1929, Carrington explained how he came to collaborate with Sylvan J. Muldoon in writing *The Projection of the Astral Body* (Rider & Co. Ltd., p. xvii). Carrington stated that in the two books mentioned above (1919, 1920) he had epitomized everything he had been able to discover concerning astral projection. He was surprised, in 1927, to receive a letter from Muldoon (then aged 25) which included the following passage: "I was much interested in your chapter on astral projection, as I have been a 'projector' for twelve years—long before I knew that anyone else in the world ever did such things. ... What puzzles me most is that you make the remark that Lancelin has told practically all that is known on the subject. Why, Mr Carrington, I have never read Lancelin's work, but if you have given the gist of it in your book, then I can write a book on the things that Lancelin does not know! ... The thing I marvel at most is that so little is said about the astral cord, the very foundation of the whole phenomenon. ... I have exteriorized enough to know that if you have given the gist of what is known, then indeed there is much darkness on the subject."

Dr Carrington suggested experiments for Muldoon to try and, two years later, they produced *The Projection of the Astral Body* in the Introduction to which Carrington said, "Mr Muldoon asserts, merely, that he has been enabled to leave his physical body at will and travel about in the present, in his immediate vicinity, in some vehicle or other, while fully conscious. This is perfectly rational, and is precisely what we should expect on the theory that these 'trips' are actual experiences. Assuming that some such entity as an Astral Body exists, and can at times be voluntarily detached from the physical body, everything else which is said falls naturally into place, and is precisely what might be expected to happen under such circumstances." He then reviewed the evidence, apart from astral projection, then available in favour of the existence of an Astral Body, namely, that based on apparitions, materializations, hauntings, etc.

In his Introduction to *The Projection of the Astral Body* (1929, p. xxv) Carrington again mentioned Prescott Hall. He said, "Several years ago, Mr Prescott Hall published, in the *Journal* of the A.S.P.R., a number of 'communications' of considerable interest, which he had received regarding the Astral Body through the instrumentality of a blind medium."[1] He added, "Their value, of course, depends altogether upon the authenticity of their source."[2] On p. 28 of that work, Muldoon referred to Hall's "work on *Astral Projection*", citing a few of the observations Hall had made when adopting the procedure recommended by the "communicators".[3] On p. 89 of *The Projection of the Astral Body* (1929) Muldoon mentioned details of a desirable diet, etc., attributing them to "Mr Prescott F. Hall",[4] i.e. overlooking the fact that they were *"communications"* and received and merely recorded by Hall (*Journal* A.S.P.R., X, 1916, p. 680).

Later, Muldoon (op. cit., 1929, pp. 101–2) said, "Here are a few suggestions for dream-plots which I have taken from Dr Carrington's *Higher Psychical Development*." What he repeated were the *"communications"*, received through Mrs Keeler, with the addition of that of a dancing flame (*Journal* A.S.P.R., 1916, p. 652).

Muldoon (pp. 19, 113) pointed out that suppressed desire is the

[1] I have made enquiries at the American S.P.R. and Mrs Keeler does not seem to have been blind.

[2] See previous footnote.

[3] No reference was given. It was not until 12 August, 1963 that, in answer to my enquiry, Laura A. Dale, the Editor of *Journal*, A.S.P.R., kindly informed me that Hall's second paper, entitled "Experiments in Astral Projection" was printed in *Journal*, A.S.P.R., XII, 1918, pp. 39–60. This is evidently what Muldoon meant by Hall's "work on *Astral Projection*".

[4] Muldoon (p. 89) says, "Mr Hall has stated ... Mr Hall is correct in his assumption that ...". But Hall was citing *"communications"*; they were not his own statements or assertions.

greatest single factor in causing projections. He used this by drinking salt water before going to sleep: the inert physical body was "incapacitated" (p. 149) but the Astral Body moved out because of the desire for a drink of water. Muldoon (p. 160) said: "See yourself becoming *conscious* just as you touch the 'glass of water'." He (p. 99) also used the "dream-control" method: e.g. imagine (so that you later tend to dream) that you are swinging (or going up in an elevator)—the Astral Body tends to do what you imagine.

The present writer published the results of a study that had occupied some five or six years entitled *The Study and Practice of Astral Projection* (Aquarian Press, 1961). Muldoon and Carrington had invited those who were sceptical concerning astral projection to prove the matter for themselves by adopting one or more of the suggested techniques. Muldoon (op. cit., 1929, p. 237) said, "Once you experience the projection of your Astral Body you will no longer doubt that the individual can exist apart from his physical body. No longer will you be forced to accept theories. No longer will you be forced to base your belief in immortality upon the word of the medium, the pastor, the Holy Books, for you will have the proof for yourself—as sure and as self-evident as the fact that you are physically alive." The present writer, on the other hand, in the Preface to his book, held that "these or any other psychic experiences should not be forced in any way. There is a time when an egg-shell can break and the chick emerge in comfort and safety." The method which he employed to determine likelihood that astral projections may involve the use of an objective Astral Body was to collect many testimonies of independent persons concerning their experiences, to classify them and to subject them to analysis. The analysis, in the main, consisted in a contrast between projections that occurred *naturally*, and therefore gradually, and those that were *enforced*, and therefore sudden (by anaesthetics, etc.).

In my book of 1961, no less than fifteen pages (pp. 145–59) were devoted to a history of astral projection. The Keeler "communications" (1916) and Hall's observations (1918) were not mentioned: I had not seen them. My method, as already said, was to analyse the testimonies of people who claimed to have had projections. In fact, apart from the references by Carrington and

Muldoon, noted above, the Keeler "communications" of 1916 do not seem to have been mentioned in the literature. They had passed into oblivion as of doubtful origin and consequently no value.

On 20 July, 1963, through the kindness of Professor Ian Stevenson, M.D., Professor and Chairman of the Department of Neurology and Psychiatry, School of Medicine, University of Virginia, U.S.A., I happened to receive a large number of copies of the *Journal* A.S.P.R. Although not a complete set, they happened to include Vol. X, 1916, with the Keeler "communications".

HALL'S ANTECEDENTS

Hall was "a thoroughgoing sceptic" concerning all psychic phenomena (including, of course, astral projections). He had two friends whom he described as "highly intelligent persons, trained in science and philosophy, practically successful in business, and superlatively sane". These people claimed to be able to leave their bodies at will to travel to non-physical regions and to converse with deceased persons there.

The sceptical Hall thought he might be able to obtain some conclusions from such matters. He argued thus: "Suppose that certain instructions *not to be found in published occult writings*, if followed by the experimenter, result in certain phenomena. Suppose that other experimenters repeat the processes and arrive at similar results. It would seem that *either a medium must have discovered the teaching or that it is supernormally communicated.*"

Hall continued, "It *so happened*[1] that a deceased friend, Miss 'X',

[1] N.B. Anyone who has had much experience of psychic work knows that these things "so happen" too frequently and significantly to be due to chance. In the present case we note that (a) Hall wanted to receive the (hitherto unpublished) techniques for astral projection and (b) none of Mrs Keeler's "communicators" ever gave similar material to anyone else. Miss "X" was merely an intermediary. She was said to be working for certain "orientals". Although, unlike her, these could not be identified, they clearly had knowledge of ancient oriental methods, Egyptian and other, that were unknown to either Hall or Keeler. Much work of this kind is done in groups. The suggestion that those chiefly responsible for the astral projection techniques were orientals (1916, p. 639) is borne out by (1) the fact that an ancient "dancing flame" method was given (1916, p. 652); (2) an Egyptian method was given (1916, p. 692); (3) an imaginary journey to the Himalayas was recommended (and produced some slight results—1916, p. 687); (4) the lily-calyx image (1916, p. 690) was used in ancient Egypt; (5) Hall "saw" an oriental figure and the head of a Hindu (1918, pp. 50, 56); (6) See 1918, p. 42, footnote regarding the meaning of the Sanskrit word "Indrya".

THE TECHNIQUES OF ASTRAL PROJECTION

began communicating at this time and offered to help in this work." The instructions would be given by her and other spirits whom she would induce to help him. This was how Hall received, from 1908–15, some 350 pages of "communications",[1] including hitherto unpublished techniques for astral projection that he gave in *Journal* A.S.P.R., X, 1916.

MRS KEELER'S ANTECEDENTS

Mrs Keeler's reading on psychic matters was very limited and does not seem to include a passing reference to, much less even a single description of, an astral projection. She was not a professional medium and used her talent (which did not involve trance) to educate her children. She took little or no interest herself in subject-matter received.

DR JAMES HYSLOP'S OBSERVATIONS

Hyslop, the famous Editor of *Journal* A.S.P.R., in 1916, said that he knew Mrs Keeler personally and "the question of fraud can be dismissed". Moreover, the "communications" were not the result of "careful education and study". He based the latter conclusion on two facts. First, her reading on psychical matters had comprised only *Intra Muros*, *The Banner of Light*, "Hudson's book" [doubtless Thomas Jay Hudson's *The Law of Psychic Phenomena*, 1893] and Dr Savage's *Life Beyond Death*. Secondly, the possibility is negatived by "the very fertility of the ideas" that the "communications" contain. He proceeded to consider what appears to be the only remaining alternative worthy of serious consideration, namely, whether they could be products of Mrs Keeler's "subconscious mind". Against that conclusion was the fact that "subconscious" fabrications "usually run up against normal experience and accepted scientific notions", whereas these "communications" are consistent enough with scientific teachings. Hyslop admitted, however, that "they cannot be confirmed by any process except cross-reference under better conditions than usually obtain". The hypothesis of "sub-conscious" invention is valueless until proved.

---

[1] I have enquired of the American S.P.R., but these 350 pages of shorthand notes, of which Hall published a "digest", are untraceable and cannot, therefore, be made to yield further possible data.

Hyslop continued, "*We shall have to work many years to ascertain just what meaning to put upon them.*" The eventual value that could be assigned to them would be based upon the fact that Mrs Keeler had certainly not obtained the ideas expressed from the reading of books, from other people, etc., and that she had not, in fact, interested herself intellectually in them at all. "The nature of the facts," said Hyslop, "does not bear the stamp of personal beliefs and edited data, as is usual in work of the kind." It is interesting to note that a practically identical observation was made, as early as 1829, by Dr J. Kerner concerning the statements made by his thirty-year-old, uneducated patient, Frau Hauffe. In *Die Seherin von Prevorst*, translated by Catherine Crowe and published in English by J. C. Moore in 1845, Kerner insisted that her "revelations" were not "portions of a system of philosophy constructed by an enlightened mind", but first-hand observations and teachings. It was important that they should be read as such.

Hyslop (p. 632) considered that *subsequent statements, similar to the Keeler "communications", from "other sources of a trustworthy character", would give the "communications" some evidential value. He explained, "And that is what is sought by us in the publication of such records." He pointed out that, while some people might consider Mrs Keeler's "communications" as confirmatory of certain of the basic teachings of eminent writers on Theosophy, Yoga, etc., "it is rather the reverse" —they may help us in determining what is acceptable in Theosophical, Anthroposophical, Yoga and other teachings.*

The *Projection of the Astral Body* was published in 1929 by Sylvan J. Muldoon and Dr Hereward Carrington (Rider & Co. Ltd.), and a second book in 1951 entitled *The Phenomena of Astral Projection* (Rider & Co. Ltd.). Muldoon published in 1936 *The Case for Astral Projection* (Aries Press). These were all works of the first importance, advancing the subject considerably. Professor Hornell Hart's classical studies appeared in *Proc.* S.P.R., 50, 1956, p. 163. Dr J. H. M. Whiteman's *The Mystical Life* was published by Faber in 1961. In the same year my book *The Study and Practice of Astral Projection* (Aquarian Press) appeared. This was described by Professor Hart (*Journal* A.S.P.R., LVI, 1962, p. 91) as "Undoubtedly the most comprehensive, systematic, and potentially epochal treatise yet to be published." We hope now to show that the possibility envisaged by Hyslop fifty years ago has matured into a high probability—that we now actually possess similar statements, from trustworthy sources, that give the Keeler "communications" "some evidential value". The corroboration of some of the basic doctrines of Theosophy, Yoga, etc., would constitute a secondary product.

This matter now assumes an importance that extends beyond the question of whether an objective body is involved in some out-of-the-body experiences, important as that is. The present writer's book, published in 1961, described, classified and analysed a hundred and sixty actual cases of astral projection, independent of "communications". We shall now determine how far the data there described agree with those given in the "communications" received half a century ago by Hall (who was quite sceptical about the matter) through the mediumship of Mrs Keeler (who had no interest in it). If our first-hand accounts correspond with what was given in these "communications", the nature of these "communicators" may well be indicated.

NOTES ON BONA FIDES

One further point may be made before we address ourselves to our task. It was not possible for the present writer to check the bona fides of a number of the people who sent in descriptions of their out-of-the-body experiences to him (*in litt.*). But he felt justified in citing them since they were identical with those published (after checking) by the S.P.R. and the deponents had not read the latter—some indeed were young folk, others unlettered folk. We may take a parallel case. Our weather forecasts are based on hundreds of reports from separate local stations, each with its own instruments. If, owing to carelessness, ignorance, or deliberate falsification, a particular station reported a barometric pressure that was markedly different from the neighbouring ones, it would not falsify the general meteorological pattern, since the error would be obvious.

It might be thought that narratives that are not corroborated are necessarily less reliable than those that have been checked. But the American expert Professor Hornell Hart (*Proc.*, S.P.R., 50, 1956, p. 241), who investigated this possibility, found that the narratives that had little evidential backing were identical with those that had much. In France, Professor C. Flammarion (*Death and its Mystery*, T. Fisher Unwin Ltd., iii, 1923, p. 113), after sixty years' experience, said, "Cases in which there was a possibility of there being concerned farceurs, liars and minds that were given to illusions ... constitute a minimum." He added, "In almost every instance in which I have been able to make a personal investigation, I have encountered perfectly trustworthy people."

The monthly periodical "British Birds" acts as a kind of watchdog in the endeavour to eliminate any possibility of false reports of birds seen in Great Britain. The number of August 1961 was devoted to certain "rarities". It had been noticed that more rare birds had been recorded from one area than from the whole of the rest of Great Britain. In 1900 only a few rare species had been recorded, but in 1904 there were thirty, in 1914 sixty-three and in 1915 fifty. All these were recorded in "British Birds", but three facts, namely, that the numbers were exceptionally high, that they were all reported in one area and that the other areas maintained approximately the same percentage of new records, caused doubts as to their validity. It now transpires that the records in question were probably deliberately recorded knowing that they were false, that they were foreign birds that had been preserved in ice. It is now practically certain that the rear end of the Grey-rumped Sandpiper has never been seen alive on these islands.

This type of deliberate falsification (which may have proved lucrative to the perpetrator) could not have its parallel in the testimonies concerning astral projection which we published in *The Study and Practice of Astral Projection* (Aquarian Press, 1961), for this was simple: it was the work of a single person who had great knowledge of the subject, whereas our testimonies are from many distinct people who had never heard of each other and none of whom benefited thereby.

The Piltdown skull, another fraudulent case, was also based on the work of one person (and in this case on a single specimen). He had great knowledge on the subject, so that his fabrication was, in fact, much what one would have expected.

Whereas the "rare birds" and the "Piltdown skull", though fraudulent, received acceptance for a time, this was because they at least fitted into the scheme of things and did not, therefore, suggest doubt. The situation is entirely different with accounts of out-of-the-body experiences. Almost everyone who hears of these cases (and has not himself had an astral projection) regards them as mere dreams. People who do have (and remember having had) the experience *thereafter, and only thereafter* are utterly convinced of its reality: they use phrases such as the following, "To my utter amazement ...", "To my astonishment ...", "Beyond worldly scepticism, beyond intellectual doubt and argument, and beyond religious dogma ..." etc.

Out-of-the-body experiences, then, are in an entirely different evidential category from the unreliable records of species of birds or the Piltdown skull. Numerous independent people who have never heard of each other, much less compared notes, make identical statements and these are identical with cases that have been carefully investigated. Discussing the value of testimony, the great logician, Archbishop Richard Whately, wrote: "When many coincide in their testimony (where no previous concert can have taken place), the probability resulting from this concurrence does not rest upon the supposed veracity of each considered separately, but on the improbability of such an agreement taking place by chance. For, though in such a case each of the witnesses should be unworthy of credit, still, *the chances would be infinite against their all agreeing in same falsehood.*"

In the physical sciences the discovery of new facts often follows the invention of new physical instruments—the microscope, the spectroscope, the telescope, radar, etc., but in psychology physical instruments are inapplicable and what is required is a new method (e.g., the dream-analysis method, word-association tests, etc.). *In "The Study and Practice of Astral Projection" we employed a contrast between the two different conditions (natural and enforced) under which "doubles" are released. In "An After-life?" we contrast the testimonies of two different kinds of people (normal or non-mediumistic, on the one hand, and mediumistic, on the other).* A third method will be employed in a forthcoming book (*Events on the Threshold of the Afterlife*) and a fourth in another (*Experiences on the Threshold of the Afterlife*). When all the books of a firm add up correctly in all directions, we rightly conclude that that firm's position is sound.

THE RELATIONSHIP BETWEEN ASTRAL PROJECTIONS AND TRANCE MEDIUMSHIP

Prescott Hall's "communicators" (1916, p. 655) made a distinction between astral projection and trance mediumship which we believe to be true and necessary. It was as follows: "Astral projection is *a positive matter*, involving a condition opposite to that of trance or [possession] mediumship. Therefore the practice of automatic writing (in which the scribe is *more or less passive, if not actually entranced*) is not favourable for astral projection."

SYSTEMATIC REVIEW OF THE "COMMUNICATIONS"

(A) BEFORE THE RELEASE OF THE "DOUBLE"

I. THE TOTAL BODILY CONSTITUTION OF MAN

THE "COMMUNICATIONS": Each mortal has, in addition to his soul and his physical body, a finer body, the "*Astral Body*" (p. 642). This is correlated with the "Astral Plane" (p. 648).

Between the physical body and the "Astral Body" is the "atmosphere", or "aura", of the physical body, then an interspace, then an astral atmosphere. The structure of the earth corresponds—it has "a general atmosphere" with an interspace "which gave rise to the idea of a river of death" (pp. 647, 659, 680).

The "physical atmosphere", which extends beyond the physical body, can be extruded and then "looks like a dark shadow" [i.e., "ghost-like"—the "ghost" of a "living" man!] Hall observed, "Apparently it is similar to what Dr W. J. Kilner (in *The Human Atmosphere*, E. P. Dutton, 1911) called 'the aura' ".[1]

"One has to go a certain distance from the physical atmosphere [= vehicle of vitality] to get in touch with other [Astral] planes" (p. 697) [i.e., the "double" is originally composite, consisting of vehicle of vitality as well as Astral Body: only when the projector's Astral Body "goes some distance from" the vehicle of vitality does the "double" become simple, consisting of Soul Body only, and he enters the Astral. This "going through", or shedding, the vehicle of vitality from the composite "double"

---

[1] According to the Foreword, "The author ... has been able to substantiate scientifically the claim made long ago by the occultists that the human body possesses a visible aura which changes its shape and size and colour according to various conditions of age and health in the individual. Dr Kilner has found that by the use of certain chemical screens, this aura may be made visible to the naked eye ... By means of the colour, size and texture of this aura, it is possible to diagnose with wonderful correctness the subject's condition of health or disease. The author offers these results ... as a very valuable aid in establishing a correct diagnosis in cases which would otherwise be doubtful." (It may be added that Wratten filter No. 36 corresponds to dicynin, the dye that Kilner used: look through this filter at daylight for half a minute, then go into a room dark enough to just see the hands.)

corresponds to "the second death" in permanent releases of the "double"—in these, the whole of the vehicle of vitality accompanies the Astral or Soul Body].

Corroborations of the "communications" by astral projectors, etc.

Hall's correlation of "the atmosphere of the physical body", "the physical atmosphere", or "the physical aura" with the human "atmosphere", or "aura", of Dr Kilner was clearly correct. It has been recognized for many centuries in almost all lands. It is the "Bardo Body" of the ancient Tibetans, the "ka" of the ancient Egyptians, the "Prânamâyakosha" (vehicle of cosmic vitality) of the ancient Hindus, the "larva" of the Romans, the "Linga Shirira" (= Sukshuma)—the "etheric double" of the Theosophists, the "nerve spirit" of German "communicators" and clairvoyants, the "vital body" of the Rosicrucians, the "somatic double" of Ralph Shirley and Prevost Battersby, the "âme vital" (vital soul), etc., and has been recognized and described by innumerable clairvoyants. W. Whately Smith (later Carington), one of our soundest psychical researchers, in a book entitled *A Theory of the Mechanism of Survival* (Kegan Paul, Trench Truber & Co., 1920, p. 160) stated: "I think it highly probable that clairvoyant descriptions of facts concerning the etheric double are often reliable." It was called "the health aura" by C. W. Leadbeater (*Man Visible and Invisible*, T.P.S., 1957), "the body of formative forces" by Dr Rudolf Steiner, "the body of electricity", "the electro-magnetic body" by others, "the Kesdjun Body" by Gurdjieff, etc. In the book by the present writer, entitled *The Supreme Adventure* (James Clarke & Co. Ltd., 1916, pp. 53, 54, 131), he employed the appropriate Hindu term, "the vehicle of vitality".

Astral projectors often describe this bodily feature and note its effect when (as commonly occurs with those in whom it is loosely associated with the physical body) part of it accompanies the extruded or projected "Astral Body": the environment then tends to be "foggy", even "watery", and these people (independently of mediums) describe the same conditions as the "dead" (necessarily through mediums), i.e., the crossing of "the river of death", in which "ghosts", and possibly "hinderers", may be encountered. They also (independently of mediums) describe the shedding of the vehicle of vitality from this composite "double" (leaving a

simple "double" consisting of the Astral, or Soul Body only), exactly as the "dead" describe shedding their vehicle of vitality (at
"the second death", usually about three days after physical death).
Examples of these matters were given in the writer's book *The
Study and Practice of Astral Projection* (Aquarian Press, 1961, pp. 14,
15, 22, 27, 40, 55, 58, 76, 93, 100, 120, 122, 136).

In his review of *The Study and Practice of Astral Projection* in *Fate*
Magazine, 1961, p. 85, David Techter said, "In his analysis, Dr
Crookall makes one very significant contribution to the under-
standing of astral projection. He presents substantial evidence
that the non-physical body is compound. ..." It will be seen that
this conception was given in 1909–18 by Mrs Keeler's "communicators" and published in 1916 independently of any systematic study of the testimonies provided by astral projectors (which,
indeed, were not then available). They said that what we call the
vehicle of vitality "can be detached from the physical body, just
as the astral can, and when it is so detached, *a person going out into
the astral can take it with him* [in which case his 'double' would be
compound, with the 'Astral' or 'Soul' Body more or less en-
shrouded] *or leave it behind"* [i.e. pass through the equivalent of
"the second death", after which process his "double" would be
simple, consisting of the unenshrouded Soul Body only].

The "river of death" corresponds to the "Hades" of the Greeks
(and Romans), the "Amenta" of the ancient Egyptians, the
"Sheol" of the Jews, the "Kama Loca" of the ancient Hindus
(and, following them, of the Theosophists), the "Bardo" of the
ancient Tibetans, "Limbo" of the Scholastic theologians, "the
lower Borderland", "Plane of Illusion", "Greylands", etc. of
various "communicators".

2. TECHNIQUES THAT FACILITATE THE RELEASE OF THE "DOUBLE"

THE "COMMUNICATIONS": (a) The withdrawal of the attention
from the physical world. The would-be projector was recommended to create mental images of lights, e.g., to concentrate on
imaginary ripples or flashes of light (p. 689).

(b) The loosening of the Astral Body from the physical body.
"Image oneself as a point in space floating, or as a piece of cloud
or as *steam"* (p. 682).

(c) The initiation of movement in the Astral Body. (1) "The image of oneself as flying" (p. 683); (2) "The image of a twirling star suspended in space" (p. 686); (3) "The attempt to visit the Himalayas in imagination" (p. 687); (4) "The image of ploughing" (p. 693); (5) "The image of rocking or of swinging" (p. 694).

(d) The release of the Astral Body from the physical body.

1. "Acquire the power to send the Astral Body out of the physical body, from which it *escapes like steam*, and to *draw it together outside*" (p. 644). When it is released naturally, it "oozes out from the physical body *from all pores* and *appears like steam* to the on-looker. After leaving, it *draws together and gradually becomes fully organized*" (p. 645).

2. "Frequent use is made of the image of a circle, or a series of circles, of smoke rings, etc." (p. 649).

3. "The image of a cone in one form or another is used because it involves the idea of *contracting to a point or expanding from a point* (e.g., passing through a water-spout or an hourglass-shaped space; constructing a cone of circles becoming smaller or larger, and turning such a cone inside out; making a revolving disc assume the form of a cone, or flattening out again to a disc" (p. 652).

4. "Concentrating upon the image of a whirlpool, or going down through a whirlpool—i.e., the principle of *contracting to a point, then expanding*" (p. 708).

5. "The image of being carried along a wave" (p. 708).

6. "The image of paying out a coil of rope, or being drawn up by means of a rope" (p. 694).

7. "The image of oneself whirling or of whirling objects—the opposite of the cone-idea. Physical whirling, like that of the Dervishes, has an effect to drive out the Astral Body, but is not a good practice. The idea of this image is to make one lose other images ... and the effect is similar to that of *being drawn out through a revolving tube*, as a rifle bullet goes out of a gun" (p. 708).

8. "Image of a tank gradually filling with water, on the top of which one floats as a point of light ... The object is to *find a small hole* in one side of the tank through which one passes out" (p. 706).

9. "The image of water ... is much used; thus, drawing water from a well; considering the physical body as a pool of water; or

dwelling on the image of a pool of water pointed in the centre" (p. 708).

10. "The mental image of a mirror is much used ... So, also the manipulation of one's own image in a mirror" (p. 690).

11. "Concentrate upon the image of the calyx of a lily" (p. 690).

12. "Steaming from limp cloth—This is often used as an image ... Sometimes it is varied by imagining that the body is a limp netting and that the Astral Body *steams* up through the holes. The idea of flatness is essential. After one has *mostly steamed out*, one is to pull instead of pushing and so *gather up* the limp cloth in one's thoughts, which has *the effect of drawing the Astral Body together*" (p. 705).

The "communicator" (p. 679) explained the rationale of these mental images in the deliberate production of astral projections: "Imagination actually creates conditions in the astral world." Again (p. 654) "What we ordinarily call 'imagination' is really exercising the astral senses. Whereas in this [physical] world, if we imagine ourselves as going to a certain city, our thought is the only result, in the astral world we should go there, at least if we wished. So, if we imagine our Astral Body as climbing out of the physical, or swinging from side to side, we have nothing as a result except the fact of our imagining; but in the astral world our thought has actually set the Astral Body in motion, although we cannot, while in the [physical] body, see that this is so. In other words, thought is creative in the astral world, and whatever we 'will' tends to be brought about." He added, "The same thing is true of the physical body, although, as the matter of which the latter is composed is more dense and has more inertia, it is harder to bring about results."

Prescott Hall (p. 644) observed: "*All the exercises for development [of astral projection] which were given me involved principles curiously suggesting what we have rationally developed as to a fourth dimension.* Images of going through an hourglass, or up a water-spout, or back of a mirror, or turning a cone inside-out, or contracting to a point and then expanding, suggest that one gets into a different space-world from that which we know." It may be added that astral projectors find that the Astral Body seems to move in a four-dimensional world and has been called "the Four-Dimensional Body".

Corroboration of the "communications" by astral projectors, etc.

The "communicators" told Hall that, in order to release his Astral Body, he should imagine certain things and explained that, so far as the Astral Body, and the Astral World, is concerned, mental images, thoughts, desires and willings are immediately creative. Sylvan J. Muldoon, the astral projector, speaking from the experience of hundreds of projections, made this latter point in his book *The Projection of the Astral Body* (Rider & Co. Ltd., 1929, p. 167) when he said, "There is a passive will and there is an active will. The passive will is the stronger; this is the will which we have when we awake in the dead of night ... We will call it the passive will because we are in a passive [hypnagogic] condition while we are using it, when we are willing in the night, conscious but drowsy—passive ... Perhaps you will say, 'What are you trying to make us believe? That one can project by merely imagining that he can?' In one sense this is truer than you might think ... The imaginative will *can* cause the projection of the Astral Body." Later (p. 212) he pointed out that in the Astral World "the mind creates its environment—yet the environment is *real*! ... It is a sort of purgatory wherein one must learn to think correctly". He continued, "This 'place' we are speaking of (I have loosely termed it 'the Astral Plane') is here upon earth, in the earth's atmosphere. Perhaps you think there is no significance in what is commonly called 'Purgatory', but that term seems very fitting for the lower Astral condition."

Yram, the French projector (*Practical Astral Projection*, Rider & Co. Ltd., p. 99), discovered the same thing for himself and said, "A thought is often enough to cause an entity which pleases or displeases to appear or disappear." Again (p. 137), "Imagination is a reality."

The "communicators" told Hall three kinds of things to imagine. The first was that "*steam*" was leaving all *the pores* of his physical body. Many astral projectors have described this phenomenon. *Psychic News*, 2 February, 1963, carried an account by Mrs Longuet of her projection. It was as follows: "I appeared to swell out of my skin and was carried by waves of *smoke-like material*." Reine, a Paris artists' model who had no education, much less knowledge of psychic matters, described to P. E.

Cornillier (*The Survival of the Soul*, Kegan Paul, Trench Trubner & Co. Ltd., 1921, pp. 3, 45, 48, 88, 95, 107, 114, 195) how her "double", which she called "*a smoke-body*", came out from her whole body, via *the pores*, but chiefly from *the head*, as "*a sort of mist, or vapour*". On a second occasion she used the words "*smoke-like*" and on a third, "*foam or mist*". Her supposed discarnate "helper", Vettellini, described the permanent release of a "double" at death (p. 462) as "like *a mist*". Mme d'Espérance (*Shadow Land*, Redway, 1897) observed that when her "double" left her body the latter was "surrounded by *a cold mist*". She observed discarnate souls who lived in a region that, to her, was "misty and cloud-like".

The second statement by Mrs Keller's "communicators" was that to image contracting to a point and then expanding, being drawn through a tube or finding a small hole in the side of a tank (all very similar symbols) would help Hall to release his Astral Body. This is clearly comparable to the "tunnel" symbol that is so often described by people who *left* their bodies. In the cases cited in *The Study and Practice of Astral Projection*, Mrs Francis Leslie (p. 8), Miss Yeoman (p. 13), Mrs Tarsikes (p. 11), Frank Lind (p. 68), Miss Bazett (p. 82), Hermione Okeden (p. 89), Mrs Bounds (p. 114) and Mrs Hatfield (p. 119) all used this term: "I seemed to float in a long *tunnel*"; "there appeared an opening, like a *tunnel*, and at the far end a light"; etc. Moreover, surely indicating that these experiences were genuine ones and not mere dreams or fantasies, many astral projectors also described the experience of "passing through" a "dark *tunnel*" (Miss Marjorie Johnson, p. 53), "*a tunnel or passageway through dark clouds*" (Percy Cole, p. 122) when their Astral Bodies, having been released from their physical bodies, *re-entered* them. Oliver Fox (*Astral Projection*, Rider & Co. Ltd.) said, "I was falling down a dark, narrow *tunnel or shaft*" and later compared the experience to "tumbling through a *hole* into a new sphere". Dr J. H. M. Whiteman (*The Mystical Life*, Faber, 1961) stated, "I seemed to pass through a *tunnel*." Miss Zoila Stables, B.A., compared the experience to "*a·long tunnel, a creek with high banks, or a long pergola*". She rightly insisted (*in litt.*): "It is too frequent a happening not to have some correspondence in reality." According to Muldoon (1929, p. 49) his sister, out of her body in sleep, "dreamed" that

she [= Astral Body] was drawn towards "*the neck* of a bottle".
These were astral projectors: they left their bodies in a *natural*
manner.

People whose Astral Bodies are *forcibly* ejected from their physical bodies by anaesthetics also compared the process to passing
through a *tunnel*. Nurse Osborn (*Light*, LV, 1935, p. 249) stated
that many patients told her that, when given the anaesthetic, they
seemed to pass down "a long *tunnel*". Ralph Shirley (*The Mystery
of the Human Double*, Rider) also recorded this fact. Mrs Hatfield
(*in litt.*) spoke of "a dark *tunnel*", while "W.E.H." (*Prediction*,
March, 1955) said, "I found myself in *an avenue of trees* slowly
moving farther and farther from my body." He added, "I continued to advance along *the avenue* towards a brilliant light at the
end of it." *Borderland*, (i, 1893-4, p. 564) carried the case of Mrs
L'Orne who used the same word as Mrs Keeler's "communicator",
namely, "*tube*": she said, "I found myself proceeding along a
straight black *tube*."

The tunnel symbol is also used by people whose Astral Bodies
separated from their physical bodies as they fell from great heights
(e.g., Douglas Bader, *Follow the Stars*).

It is also used by mediums to describe the evacuation of the
physical body by the Astral Body, preparatory to the latter being
temporarily entered ("possessed") and used by the discarnate
"communicator": thus Mrs Piper spoke of "a dark *tunnel*" (Alta
Piper, *The Life and Work of Mrs Piper*, Kegan Paul, Trench
Trubner & Co. Ltd., p. 115).

The third statement by Mrs Keeler's "communicators" was that
Hall would loosen his Astral Body from its immersion in the
physical body if he imagined that he was rocking, swinging,
whirling, floating or moving towards the Himalayas—that these
activities tended to be thus initiated in the Astral Body. The astral
projector S. J. Muldoon (op. cit., 1929, p. 27) described these as
"the 'elementary stages' of astral projection". The words "*rocking*", "*swinging*", "*floating*" etc., commonly occur in the descriptions given by numerous other astral projectors.

3. BREATHING TECHNIQUES

"Breathing is important, as the pulse in the brain is synchronous
with it. Therefore various breathing exercises ... For getting out

of the body, *holding the breath* is of value, but holding it out has no effect" (p. 649).

Corroboration of the "communications" by astral projectors, etc.

Mrs Keeler's "communicators" (whose statements were published in America in 1916) said that *holding* the breath tended to release the Astral Body from the physical body. In Sweden the clairvoyant Emanuel Swedenborg (1688–1772), who had many out-of-the-body experiences, wrote (in Latin) in his "Spiritual Diary", "Retaining or *holding-back* the breath is equivalent to having intercourse with the *soul*, drawing it with the body." There is, of course, a whole literature in Yoga on *holding* the breath (= "prana-yama") and its possible psychic effects. [Yoga breathing exercises should be avoided in the absence of a competent (clairvoyant) teacher, for they can be definitely dangerous]. In Richard Wilhelm's book entitled *The Golden Flower, A Chinese Book of Life* (meaning super-physical life), published by Routledge & Kegan Paul in 1931, representing esoteric Taoist teachings that date back to the eighth century and were printed in Chinese in 1920, the would-be astral projector is told that the breathing must be rhythmical, advice that applies to all kinds of psychic work. Mrs Eileen J. Garrett made important observations on the effect of breathing on psychic abilities in her book entitled *Telepathy* (Creative Age Press Inc., 1941, pp. 40, 51, 59–60, 103, 104 et seq., 128–9, 192), in *Awareness* (Creative Age Press Inc., 1943, pp. 17, 45, 90, 92, 116, 135–6, 138) and in *Adventures in the Supernormal* (Garrett Publications Inc., 1949, pp. 7, 143, 164, 165–6). These matters are beyond conjecture. In 1930 Dr E. Osty, the French physician who followed Geley as Director of the Institute Metaphysique Internationale, Paris, experimented with Rudi Schneider (*La Revue Métapsychique*, 1932) and obtained noteworthy results. An object, such as a handkerchief, was placed on the laboratory table to see if Rudi could move it by supernormal means. The object was protected by a beam of infra-red light focused on a photo-electric cell. If anything interrupted this beam, a bell rang (after the manner of a burglar-alarm). During certain experiments the bell did ring, and, as had been arranged, ultra-violet light flooded the room and a camera automatically photographed the whole scene. The photographs proved that the obscuration of the beam had not been brought about by Rudi's arm or leg (which, in any case, was held by the experimenters) but by something — ectoplasm, the "semi-physical" substance that is sometimes given out from the vehicle of vitality that was normally invisible.

Now Rudi's breathing was normally 12–14 per minute, but during these experiments (when he was in trance, i.e., with the Astral Body exteriorized) it was 120–300 per minute (and very noisy). When the alarm-bell was replaced by suitable instruments, Osty found that *the vibration-rate of the* (?) *ectoplasm was always exactly twice Rudi's rate of breathing. Moreover, the greatest emissions of* (?) *ectoplasm were under the control of Rudi's will—they occurred after he had said they would occur. The* (?) *ectoplasm was not only "semi-physical" but also "semi-mental", because "biddable": it was intermediate between matter and mind.*

4. THE EFFECT OF STUDY AND CONCENTRATION

"Every living being sends out vibrations; but those of spirits are faster than those of mortals. The latter can by study and concentration, however, accelerate theirs" (p. 707).

Corroboration of the "communications" by astral projectors, etc.

Little need be said about this: it is well known. Mary E. Monteith (*The Fringe of Immortality*, John Murray, 1920, p. 40) learned that "Psychic development depends more on concentration than on anything else—not practised artificially, but habitually on every little thing in daily life." One of the best books on this is published by The Buddhist Lodge, London, under the title *Concentration and Meditation* (1943): its title-page has this quotation from "Dhammapada"—"You yourself must make the effort: Buddhas do but point the Way."

5. CONDITIONS FAVOURABLE TO PROJECTION

The position of the physical body—"Sit sufficiently *erect* so that the circulation is not interfered with, for blood-pressure is an important factor" (p. 643). "*Crossing the hands and feet is bad* ... as it mixes up *the nerve currents* and hinders the exit of the Astral Body" (p. 679). "Darkness and closing the eyes make the nerves more sensitive. In fact, it is not common for a person to get out the first time with the [physical] eyes open" (p. 679).

Incidental aids—"A dish of water near one sitting" is recommended—or "the vapour of water" or "putting one's hands in water" (p. 708). This "keeps away objectionable and evil personalities" [= possible "hinderers"].

Food—"Abstain from meat" (p. 643). "Fasting may be useful, while over-eating, especially near the time of making experiments, is an absolute bar to success" (p. 643). "Fasting often helps to liberate the Astral Body" (p. 681). "Do not eat just before an experiment in projection—it interferes with the circulation of the blood" (p. 680).

"Dulling drugs, such as anaesthetics, alcohol and tobacco, affect the circulation of the blood and therefore projection" (p. 649). "Tobacco draws noxious influences and puts undesirable products into the blood stream, but its chief evil is that it interferes with good spirits [= possible 'helpers'] and interferes with their approach" (p. 706).

Eat a vegetable diet. "Fruit and vegetables make the blood able to attract spiritual influences [= possible 'helpers']. Carrots are also beneficial. Raw eggs are favourable" (p. 680).

"Nuts, especially peanuts, are bad" (p. 680).

"Liquids are beneficial (for the development of astral projection) but too much liquid thins the blood and alters the circulation" (p. 680).

"After five or six months of development ... advanced persons can eat anything" (p. 681).

Corroboration of the "communications" by astral projectors, etc.

These are all mentioned by numerous astral projectors on the basis of their own personal observations. For instance, the desirability of fasting, the undesirability of crossing the hands and feet and the value of water were mentioned by Reine, the French sensitive of P. R. Cornillier (op. cit., 1921, pp. 40, 122, 188, 279, 288, 349, 387 respectively). An astral projector wrote to *The London Forum* and said that the feet should be uncrossed. Reine found that "warm and damp" weather conditions prevented satisfactory results (p. 349).

(B) THE CONTRAST BETWEEN *NATURAL* AND *ENFORCED* RELEASES

MRS KEELER's "communicators" (1916) said, "*Anaesthetics* blow the soul and spirit forcibly out of the body, hence the person feels no pain. But, as they affect the physical circulation and the blood contains much of the 'physical atmosphere or aura' [i.e., the vehicle of vitality], *they have the effect of dulling the astral senses also, so he does not have astral consciousness and rarely perceives anything while out*" (p. 683). Again (p. 683): "In the case of getting out by the action of *anaesthetics, the astral senses are dulled*, so that the person rarely perceives anything while out, or remembers it." Still again (p. 698) the "communicators", in America, described the ["nerve-] soul" (i.e., the vehicle of vitality) much like the German clairvoyant, Frau Hauffe, had described it in 1829—as "*a substance*" *that is "attached to certain nerve centres" and is "blown out quickly with the Astral Body by an accidental blow or by anaesthetics*", i.e., when the release of the "double" is *enforced*.

On pp. 645, 646 the "communicators" mentioned two possible methods of *natural* release of the "double". In the first, it "*oozes out from the physical body from all its pores and appears like steam to the onlooker. After leaving the body it draws together and gradually becomes fully organized* ..." In the second method the "double" withdraws from *the lower extremities* of the physical body, "resting for a time on the nerves of *the stomach*, rises to *the throat* and finally passes out of the top of *the head*. It can also be only *partially* extruded—from any part of the physical body—"like an arm or hand".

Corroboration of the "communications" by astral projectors, etc.

Taking the last-mentioned description first; as we have already said, the French sensitive, Reine (op. cit., 1921, pp. 20, 136), exactly matched this when she described the release of her own Astral Body—it left her "whole body", but "chiefly by *the head*, by all *the pores, like a mist, vapour or foam*" which gathered together as a mass at some distance from her body. The other method of exit was described by some astral projectors: thus, the Revd. Bertrand's Astral Body first withdrew from *the lower extremities* and finally departed via *the head* (see *The Study and Practice of Astral Projection*, 1961, p. 6).

As already said, the contrast between natural and enforced releases of the "double" was the chief method which the present writer (who had not then seen the Keeler "communications") used in an endeavour to determine whether or not the descriptions of the deponents represented genuine out-of-the-body experiences. Before this (from 1952 to 1957) he had used the same method in investigating "communications" from the supposed dead concerning their final projection, i.e., death, and these he had published in *The Supreme Adventure* (James Clarke, 1961). He began *The Study and Practice of Astral Projection* (p. 1) as follows: "The writer has studied the supposed experiences of people who had left the body *permanently*, i.e., died: he found that those who said that they died *naturally* described one series of experiences while those who said their death was *enforced* described another, a more restricted, series (Appendix V). Some of the 'dead' gave explanations of these differences. Their explanations are reasonable. Moreover, in some cases, they agree with the findings of psychical science. We therefore conclude that the accounts of the after-death experiences which we examined are very probably, indeed almost certainly, genuine. ... The present book analyses the experiences of people who claim to leave the body *temporarily*. It is found that those who did so *naturally* typically describe one set of experiences, while those whose exteriorisation was *enforced* typically describe another, a more restricted series. It is further found that there is a remarkable correspondence between the accounts of those who claimed to leave the body permanently and those who claimed to leave it only temporarily. This correspondence in independent narratives seems explicable only if both sets of narratives are substantially true. No alternative explanation seems possible."

After citing and analysing the hundred and sixty cases of projection, contrasting the natural cases with those that were enforced, I concluded (p. 142): "We suggest that in those temporary exteriorizations which are *enforced* much of the 'body-veil' (= vehicle of vitality) is ejected from the body and that it more or

less effectively enshrouds the Psychical or Soul [= Astral] Body.
Hence those who are forced out of their bodies by anaesthetics,
etc. typically *either* remain on earth *or* enter 'Hades' (dream) conditions. We suggest that in those temporary exteriorizations which
occur *naturally* only a little of the vehicle of vitality, or 'body-veil',
goes out with the Psychical or Soul Body ..."

A further corroboration of the Keeler "communications" concerning the "double" appearing to leave the body like *"steam"*
comes from numerous observers at deathbeds. Lily Price, J.P., of
Hanover Street, Rozelle, N.S.W., Australia, sent the following to
the writer (*in litt.*) "I saw *a mist* rise from the (dying) girl's *head.*
The mist gradually took the shape of the child's bodily form ..."
Florence Marryat (*The Spirit World*, F. V. White, 1894) observed,
"A film, *like a cloud of smoke*, gathered above her *head*. It spread out
and acquired the shape of the girl's body ..." The Revd. G.
Maurice Elliott and his wife (*Angels Seen Today*, 1919, p. 123) saw,
"Just above the bed *a white hazy mist* which grew larger. In a short
while it took the perfect form of the suffering one." J. C. Street
(*The Hidden Way*) stated: "A thin violet *column of vapour* was observed to leave the dying body and collect above it ..." "Mr G",
whose case was published by the S.P.R. (*Journ.* XIII, 1908, p. 368)
saw *"clouds"* leave his dying wife's body. His doctor said that "a
state of hallucinatory insanity" was out of the question: Moreover, "Mr G" had "read nothing in the occult line". Dozens of
similar cases could be cited.

Mrs Keeler's "communicators" (p. 683) stated, *"The going-out
may be while a person is unconscious (as in sleep)*; but if it is accom-
plished consciously, the person simply has his consciousness
doubled and functions upon two planes at once [= 'dual consciousness'] ... It is usually in an *upward* direction, away from the
earth. *A person may get out without knowing it and in that case the test
is whether he can see his physical body.*" Again (p. 692) "The sight of
the physical body is one of the first eviden ces of being out."

Corroboration of the "communications" by astral projectors, etc.

Many of the astral projectors whose experiences are cited in
The Study and Practice of Astral Projection (e.g., Mrs Land, p. 23, a
lady, p. 39, Mrs Leonard, p. 42, J. H. Dennis, p. 48, Miss Newby,
p. 51, Horace Leaf, p. 60, Mrs Roberts, p. 70, Wm. E. Edwards,

p. 73, Dr Ostby, p. 88, etc.) described how they awoke from sleep to find their Astral Bodies free from their physical bodies. This fact is to be correlated with the advice given by the "communicators" (and by Muldoon), that the best time to project is after one has been to sleep, say about 3 a.m. (when the physical body is in the maximum state of relaxation).[1]

---

[1] The contrast between *natural* and *enforced* releases of "doubles" was also mentioned in "*communications*" received in England by the Hon. Ralph Shirley and published in *The Mystery of the Human Double* (Rider & Co. Ltd., p. 119). They were from a supposed discarnate Professor whom Shirley had "more than ordinary reason" to accept as genuine. The "Professor" stated that (1) the consciousness of the anaesthetized person is "not normal" but "confused and vague" and (2) that his environment is not that which is entered in deep natural sleep [= "Paradise", corresponding to the Soul or Astral Body], but "a veritable world of ghosts" [= "Hades", corresponding to the vehicle of vitality]. The "Professor" added that the anaesthetized person is "pulled back much more sharply" into the physical body (as well as being pushed out of it "much more rapidly") than if these operations are natural. This is doubtless because his released double includes some of the vehicle of vitality (which will not go far from the physical body).

(C) THE RELEASE OF THE "DOUBLE" (ASTRAL BODY)—MENTAL FEATURES

I. THE "BLACKOUT" CAUSED BY THE RELEASE

MRS KEELER'S "communicators" (pp. 652, 655, 683) stated that, at the moment the Astral Body is released from the physical body, "*there is a moment of unconsciousness—and the same in returning*". Again, "The going out from the body may be ... in full consciousness *except for the instant when the soul changes its centre from the physical to the astral*." Still again, "At the moment of the separation of the two bodies *there is usually a moment of unconsciousness*."

Corroboration of the "communications" by astral projectors, etc.

This remarkable statement is borne out by the numerous testimonies of independent astral projectors cited in *The Study and Practice of Astral Projection* (1961): it is, we suggest, related to the experience that was mentioned above (p. 7) as like passing through a dark tunnel with a light at the other end—the latter was merely a fairly long "blackout". (We have suggested that the "blackout" of consciousness is due to the fact that, during the brief period of separation, neither the Astral Body nor the physical body was available as an instrument of consciousness.) Of the projectors whose testimonies were given in our book, Mrs McDowell (p. 22) said, "I 'blacked-out' at the same distance from my body when I approached it", i.e., she observed the experience both when she left the body and when she re-entered it. In some cases it is so brief or slight as to pass unnnoticed: hence some of the projectors reported the experience when *they left the body only* (e.g., Blakeley, p. 3, Yeoman, p. 13, Brooks, p. 55, Kaeyer, p. 57, René C., p. 83, Cripps, pp. 92, 167, Funk's friend, p. 91, Anon., p. 117, Symonds, p. 123, lady of Dallas, p. 126), others only *when they re-entered their bodies only* (e.g., Mrs Dowell, p. 22, lady, p. 39, Miss Johnson, p. 54, Hives, p. 60, Addison, p. 98, Carrington's friend, p. 115, Hymans, p. 120, Hotel guest, p. 131). But still others observed and recorded tne experience *both when they left and when they re-entered their bodies* (e.g., Kelley, pp. 4, 5, Mme d'Espérance, pp. 39, 41). Among those who described going out through "*a dark tunnel*" were Leslie (p. 8), Mrs Tarsikes, (p. 11), Yeoman (p. 68), Lind (p. 68), Bazett (p. 82), Okeden (p. 89), Bounds (p. 114), Hatfield (p. 19), while among those who describe it on the re-entry were Johnson (p. 53) and Cole (p. 122).

2. "DUAL CONSCIOUSNESS"

This has already been mentioned. According to Mrs Keeler's "communicators" (pp. 653, 656, 657) an astral projector, i.e., a man whose Astral Body is loosened from and about to leave the physical body, "may see spirits before he has actually succeeded in getting out". (They also stated that, "To see a spirit in the early stages of development of astral projection requires the co-opera-tion of spirits"—p. 656). This awareness of two "worlds", the physical and another ("Hades" if "semi-physical", "Paradise" if "super-physical"), involving the use, either simultaneously or suc-cessively, of both the physical body and the Astral Body, is called "dual consciousness". Further, the fact that both those whose Astral Bodies are partially released *temporarily* and those who are leaving it *permanently* may see into "the next world" suggests that those who are in that world ("spirits") can see the partially-released Astral Bodies (of astral projectors and the dying): it is presumably a two-way activity.

The "communicators" (p. 655) said, "As a person begins to develop [astral projection], his radiations become more luminous (because until then the luminosity of his Astral Body, enmeshed in the grosser physical body, has been quenched) and this fact attracts the attention of spirits, both good and bad. The former try to assist him and the latter to hinder him in his efforts." Later (p. 650) the "communicators" said, "The degree of development attained (in getting the Astral Body free from the physical) at any time is manifested by the radiations of the physical and Astral bodies. In an undeveloped person these go out at right angles from the body; when a person is more developed they tend to point upwards. They should also be evenly distributed all round the body." Still later (p. 690) they stated, "Masters are advanced spirits who are especially occupied in helping the development of [astral projection in] mortals. They then instruct and help the mortals in ways otherwise impossible." Again (p. 656): "No two persons develop in precisely the same way and even assisting spirits cannot tell what the next step will be, although they are usually told by more advanced spirits what the ultimate will be, for *all assistance is directed by the more advanced spirits who give the guides directions from time to time.*" On p. 657 we find, "The guiding spirits can help in development and not only by instructions but by charging the person with force and helping to pull the Astral [Body] out." On p. 658: "The birth of the Astral [Body] is not unlike a physical birth or the coming out of a butterfly from a chrysalis."

Corroboration of the "communications" by astral projectors, etc.

Examples of "dual consciousness", described by astral projectors, are given in *The Study and Practice of Astral Projection* and, as might be expected, if the "communicators" are right and the "astral senses" are "dulled" when projection is enforced by anaesthetics, only one (Hartmann, p. 128) is of the *enforced* type. The phenomenon was described in *natural* projections by Geddes (p. 16), Fox (p. 25), Huntley (p. 36), Mrs Leonard (pp. 42, 67), Van Eeden (p. 83), Mrs "H.F.P." (p. 107) and Mrs Tarsikes (p. 161).

Dual consciousness is said in "communications" other than those that came through Mrs Keeler to often occur in the course of transition, hence deathbed visions (see *The Supreme Adventure*, pp. 20, 100, 101, 137, 142, 178). In a report on Deathbed Observations by Physicians and Nurses (Parapsychological Monographs No. 3, 1961) by Dr K. Osis the facts supported the "communications"—Dr Osis said, "As a rule the dying see visions with clear consciousness"—they are not morbid or delirious: moreover, they see twice as many "dead" people as "living" ones (whereas, according to two British investigations, "living" people see twice as many "living" as "dead" ones). Dr Osis pointed out that the odds against this being due to chance are astronomical.

3. DISCARNATE "HINDERERS" AND "HELPERS"
(= "DELIVERERS")

The Keeler "communicators" have already been noted as saying that spirits see the increasing luminosity of the Astral Bodies of those who are developing astral projection, that good spirits try to help but evil ones try to hinder the person concerned. These "communicators", like astral projectors themselves, recognize that a projected "double" may include some of the substance of the vehicle of vitality, which corresponds to "Hades" conditions (as well as the Astral Body which corresponds to "Paradise" conditions). In that event "hinderers" may be encountered. Mrs Keeler's "communicators" (p. 660) said, "Jealous spirits can throw a coarse aura around a person so as to shut out light so that he sees less." Sometimes, "everything seems black". Some "hinderers" may be seeking physical sensations which they cannot satisfy in their present environment and without a physical body (hence astral projectors should avoid alcohol, drugs and tobacco). But once a projector has "reached a certain stage of development, bad spirits have no power over him" (p. 700). Later (p. 704) they said that the projector can reach a state that is normal to advanced spirits—when "his vibrations are too strong to be borne by evil spirits and he is able to protect himself as his guides had hitherto protected him". (On p. 707 they observed, "Lower spirits cannot endure the vibrations of very high spirits.")

"Hinderers" can "prevent" the release and rising of the Astral Body, can cause the projector to have "discordant feelings" and can "kindle fires to divert his attention" from "deliverers" and conditions in the "Paradise" environment which he is on the verge of entering (p. 703).

Mrs Keeler's "communicators" stated (p. 703) that astral projection is different from trance mediumship and that "guides", or "helpers", in the development of astral projection, are "of a different kind" from the "controls" or "guides" who help in the transmission of message. They said that those who help with the development of an astral projector "may hold frequent consultations among themselves as to the best course for him to pursue and may consult the higher intelligences in regard thereto".

The "communicators" said that "helpers" usually assist in the release of the Astral Body from its physical counterpart, "at least the first time" (p. 683), i.e., they act as "deliverers", the equivalents of earthly midwives, since the release of the Astral Body from the physical is very like the birth of a baby from the body of its mother.

Some "helpers" may assist a projector by using the same techniques as some "hinderers". They "stop the rising of his Astral

Body if it is going too far" (p. 702). The projector "at first tends to go too far" from his body because he has still to learn to estimate "distances" in the Astral World and in such cases he may be "stopped by the guides who erect a screen of heavy vibrations in his path" (p. 679).

"Helpers" may find it necessary to "use an illness, or some other extreme influence, to break the connexion [attraction] between the [Astral and physical] bodies" (p. 680). (With regard to this matter, as with almost all others mentioned by Mrs Keeler's "communicator", "Vettellini", the "communicator" of P. E. Cornillier, op. cit., 1921, p. 86, is in agreement).[1]

Corroboration of the "communications" by astral projectors, etc.

"Hinderers" are mentioned by many astral projectors as encountered when their "doubles" were relatively dense, i.e., included much of the vehicle of vitality, conditions which they usually "passed through". Vincent Turvey (1909, p. 210) reported "impersonating entities". Oliver Fox (*Astral Projection*, Rider & Co. Ltd., p. 48) on one occasion felt certain stresses and stated, "I had a sense of invisible, intangible powers which caused this." On another occasion (p. 19) he saw "a grinning face" and heard "mocking voices". Muldoon (1929, pp. 216–7), out of his body in a relatively dense "double", encountered "F.D.", an "earthbound" soul who tried to attack him. In France, Yram (*Practical Astral Projection*, Rider & Co. Ltd., pp. 80, 101, 103, 105, 107) described the same techniques of hindrance as Mrs Keeler's "communicators" had done in America—they tried to "hem him in" and (p. 144) "mocked" him.

The above were all astral projectors. People whose "doubles" were released from their bodies in hypnotic trance make the same statements.

Cornillier's sensitive, Reine (op. cit., 1921, pp. 8, 34), described

---

[1] One often hears people make the statement, "It is God's will that you are healthy, therefore ..." But if illness can be used to one's advantage, as these "communicators", one in America and the other in France, suggest, then the matter is not so simple as many suppose.

[2] Some "hinderers" and some "helpers" may not be entities distinct from the person concerned: they may be personifications of his own fears, hopes, etc. But even so, "hinderers" are chiefly encountered in the early and "lower" stages, "helpers" in the later and "higher" stages.

the "hinderers" as using the same technique as Mrs Keeler's "communicators" (in America) and the astral projector Yram (in France): she said that they "held her up" by "surrounding" her newly-released "double" and they "formed a barrier" in an attempt to prevent her leaving these ("Hades") conditions and entering satisfactory ("Paradise") conditions. Moreover, they "mocked" her (pp. 8, 18).

"Helpers" were mentioned by many astral projectors whose testimonies were cited in *The Study and Practice of Astral Projection*: they included Dorothy Peters (p. 48), Mrs Sheridan (p. 70), Dr Hout (p. 77), Wirt (p. 81), Miss Bazett (p. 82), Pelley (p. 95), Miss Addison (p. 97), Dr Enid Smith (p. 120), Mrs Cripps (p. 166) and Sculthorpe (p. 172). Miss Addison (loc. cit.) heard one "helper" say to another, "Let her return now slowly and next time she will not be afraid." There are several independent cases in which this sort of procedure was reported. Muldoon (1929, p. 76) observed, "Friends in the invisible realm can, and many times *do*, lend a helping-hand ..." Fox was told (mentally) by a helper not to be afraid. Reine received all kinds of help—to leave the body, to make clear observations while out of it, etc.

The observations of Lily M. Price, of Hanover Street, Rozelle, N.S.W., Australia, have already been mentioned: "I was watching by the bedside—I saw the child's grandmother appear ... She began to move her hands as if she were trying to gently draw something outwards and upwards from the child's *head*. The mist gradually took on shape of the girl's bodily form. All the while the grandmother's hands were moving in a cupping fashion—*just as a nurse might try to help a physical child to be born* ..." The grandmother helped as a "deliverer".

(D) THE RELEASE OF THE "DOUBLE" (ASTRAL BODY)—BODILY FEATURES

1. THE PROCESS IS AN INDIVIDUAL ONE

THE "COMMUNICATIONS": "No two persons develop in precisely the same way" (p. 654).

Corroboration of the "communications" by astral projectors, etc.

Muldoon (op. cit., 1929, p. 186), after describing various stages in the development of projection, stated, "Nothing which I have said is invariably true ..."

2. EXIT IS OFTEN CHIEFLY VIA THE HEAD

THE "COMMUNICATIONS": The Astral Body "starts to rise from the large nerves back of the *solar plexus*; from there it rises to *the throat*, and finally passes out at the top of *the head*. Although this is the normal course and that which occurs at death, a person, with practice, can send the Astral out from *any part* of his physical body, and can cause it to leave *all parts of the body at once, oozing out like steam* and drawing together outside".

Corroboration of the "communications" by astral projectors, etc.

Many of the astral projectors whose testimonies were cited in *The Study and Practice of Astral Projection* said that they left via the head: this applied to Miss Blakeley (pp. 3, 4), Dr Wiltse (p. 5), Bertrand (p. 6), Molly Fancher (p. 21), Fox (p. 26), Mrs "M.A.E." (p. 47), Dorothy Peters (p. 47), Helen Brooks (p. 56), Mr Leaf (p. 61), Mrs Roberts (p. 86), Mrs H. D. Williams (p. 94), Miss Addison (p. 98), Mrs Cripps (p. 166), Muldoon (p. 167) and Mrs Joy (pp. 174, 175).

A number of projectors describe the second method that was mentioned by the "communicators", i.e., oozing out. For example, Reine the unlettered sensitive of Cornillier (op. cit., 1921, p. 20), said that her "fluidic body" "came out from her whole body as a sort of mist or vapour" and collected above her. Another of her descriptions (p. 136), given in France, is practically identical with that of the Keeler "communicators" in America: her "fluidic body" came out "from all over the body ... by all the pores, like a foam or mist, and formed into a mass at some distance". (We have cited several other such cases in another book, entitled *An After-Life?* and there suggested that these are mediumistic people, having relatively loose vehicles of vitality.)

3. THE COURSE OF RELEASE IS OFTEN SPIRAL

THE "COMMUNICATIONS": "In leaving the physical, [the Astral Body] usually goes out in a zig-zag or spiral movement, but afterwards travels in a straight line" (pp. 646, 683). Again, "The Astral Body often leaves the physical in a spiral path" (p. 698).

Corroboration of the "communications" by astral projectors, etc.

In *The Study and Practice of Astral Projection*, Einarsson (p. 21) ascended "slantingly", both Rebell (p. 62) and Betty White (p. 139) used the word "obliquely", Sculthorpe (p. 66) said "at a tangent", while Mrs D. Parker (p. 128) observed "a spiral spin". We suggest that, in the early stage of its release, the Astral Body often contains a substantial portion of the "semi-physical" vehicle of vitality and is, therefore, influenced by the physical body that it has just left. It should be noted that the "communicators" make use of this spiral course in an exercise to induce projection (if one *imagines* the Astral Body spiralling out, it definitely tends to do so). Muldoon (op. cit., p. 15) pointed out that the first projection of A. J. Davis was induced by a hypnotist and his Astral Body "moved through the air in a spiral direction". Muldoon's book *The Case for Astral Projection* (Aries Press, 1936, p. 24) says, "Sometimes the phantom projects in a 'spiral spin'." Later, Muldoon and Carrington (*The Phenomena of Astral Projection*, Rider, 1951) cited several examples of the phenomenon. On p. 63 is mentioned "the spiral spin": on p. 57 "spinning like an aeroplane propeller"; and on pp. 175, 213, "whirling".

Independent observation of the spiral course comes from clairvoyant observers of transitions. For example, Mrs Eileen J. Garrett (*My Life as a Search for the Meaning of Mediumship*, Rider, 1939, p. 26) observed "a grey smoke-like substance, rising in spiral form" from dying ducks and later (p. 90) a similar phenomena when her own child died—the substance "curled and floated rhythmically", and disappeared.

4. THE EFFECT OF INERTIA

THE "COMMUNICATIONS": "After getting out, it is necessary to learn to stay still in one place because the person [Astral Body] tends to continue in motion and therefore sees other things in motion which are really at rest. Hence, he cannot see spirits in their true dimensions, or the true relations between objects, until he himself is stationary. He should not attempt to touch anything he sees or he may get tangled up with it and have his poise affected" (p. 659). Again, (p. 679), "The power to stay in one place and to estimate the distance one has gone is important. Before the locality-function has been acquired, the person may feel a loss of will and of identity, due to confusion as to his whereabouts." The "communicator" said (p. 649) that "Looking at a bright object is sometimes used, not for hypnotic effect, but to steady a person in space."

Corroboration of the "communications" by astral projectors, etc.

Muldoon (1929, p. 28) referred to "a fundamental law of astral projection"—if a person (in normal waking state) is walking round and comes up against some barrier, this stops the physical body, but the Astral Body "keeps on moving in the given direction for a moment", i.e., there is a tendency, slightly and momentarily, to project the Astral Body by using inertia.

5. THE "SILVER CORD" EXTENSION

THE "COMMUNICATIONS": Mrs Keeler's "communicators" (pp. 646, 654, 684, 708) mentioned *"an elastic cord"* or *"the vital nerve"* (correctly correlated by Hall with "the silver cord" of Ecclesiastes [xii, 6]). They said, "The Astral Body, when out, is connected with the physical body by an elastic cord, which is sufficient connexion to *enable the vital processes of the physical body* to continue." If astral travel is to take place, this "cord" must be made elastic, "so as to *follow* the person in his flight"—[i.e., the "cord" is essentially *an extension* of the forward-moving Astral Body—it is *behind* under these circumstances and may not, therefore, be seen by the projector].

Corroboration of the "communications" by astral projectors, etc.

In the astral projections that were cited in *The Study and Practice of Astral Projection*, the "silver cord" was described as having been seen by Dr Wiltse (p. 5), Bertrand (p. 6), the Countess of Tankerville (p. 8), Mrs Tarsikes (p. 11), Ogden (p. 15), Muldoon (p. 18), Turvey (p. 20), Fox (p. 25), Gerhardi (pp. 27, 29, 30, 31), Home (p. 33), Huntley (p. 36), Mrs Leonard (pp. 43, 44), Miss "P.L." (p. 47), Brunton (p. 50), Helen Brooks (p. 56), Mrs Larsen (p. 56), Sigrid Kaeyer (p. 57), Leaf (p. 61), Rebell (p. 62), Sculthorpe (p. 66), Mrs Boorman (p. 71), W. E. Edwards (pp. 73, 172), Mrs Garrett (p. 80), Wirt (p. 81), Mrs Alice Gilbert (p. 82), Tibetans (pp. 85, 86), Bulford (p. 90), Mrs Cripps (pp. 92, 116), Mrs H. D. Williams (p. 94), Anon. lady (p. 129), Mrs "T.D." (p. 114), Carrington's friend (p. 116), the Prodigal (p. 117), Stuart-Young (p. 127), Crabbe (p. 133), Dr Hout (p. 134), Mrs Tarsikes (p. 161), Mrs "Prothero" (p. 173), Miss Roberts (p. 174), Mrs Joy (p. 175), Dr Simons (p. 178).

The "silver cord" is not a physical feature. It was likened by Bertrand to "a kind of *elastic* string", by Muldoon to "an *elastic-like* cable", by Turvey to "a spider's cord" which was "*silver*" and which "extends and contracts as an *elastic* cord", by Gerhardi to "a coil of *light*", "a *lighted* cord", "a thin *ray of light*" and "the *silver* cord" (which he observed was *behind* his Astral Body as he moved forward.) Home likened his to "*a silvery-like light*", Huntley described "a feeble *thread*", Miss "P.L." "a cord", Mrs Larsen "*a current* of mysterious influence", Sigrid Kaeyer "*a connexion*".

Rebell described "a thin *luminous* ribbon", Mrs Boorman "a *stream* of *light*", Wirt "a *silver* cord or chain", Mrs. Gilbert "a cloudy-looking cord", the Tibetans "a strand or cord", Mrs Cripps "a shaft of *sunlight*", Stuart-Young "a *thread*", the Anon. lady "a beam of *light*", Mrs "T.D." "a smoky string", Mrs "Prothero" "a slender, *slightly luminous* cord", Dr Simons "an *elastic* force", etc.

These people who independently gave such similar descriptions of what they saw include Britons, Americans, Frenchmen, Tibetans, Latvians, etc., clergymen, doctors, authors, musicians, etc. Many of them had never heard of the Astral Body or of astral projection.

On account of both its appearance and its function, "the silver cord" was compared by a number of astral projectors with the umbilical cord of childbirth.

The fact that the cord is an extension is clearly shown when the numerous testimonies of astral projectors that were cited in *The Study and Practice of Astral Projection* are examined. First we note that the English soldier whose experience was published by G. B. Crabbe (p. 151) exclaimed, "I *came down* that silver cord and returned to the old body", while Mrs M. Hutchinson (*in. litt.*) stated, "I found a kind of pipeline which *guided me back* to my body", and Mrs Elizabeth Gaythorpe (*in. litt.*) ".returns *down* a long steep road (the cord?)"; Mrs Piper, in America, returning to her body after being "out" in trance, said "I *came in* on a cord, a silver cord" (Sir Oliver Lodge, *The Survival of Man*, Methuen, 1909, p. 276); the "communicator" of Fr. Greber in Germany (*Communication with the Spirit World*, Felsberg, 1932, p. 111) stated, "It is *along* this band of od that the spirit finds its way back into the body of the medium." These and other considerations leave little doubt that the "silver cord" is, in fact, *an extension*. The conditions under which the various astral projectors reported having seen their own "silver cords" accord with this conception: (1) if the released Soul Body is rising above the physical body, the "cord" will be seen *when the person concerned looks down*; this was described by Bertrand (p. 6), Fox (p. 25), Brunton (p. 50), Mrs Boorman (p. 71), Mrs "Prothero" (p. 131) etc.; (2) if the released Soul Body is moving forward, away from the physical body, the "cord" will be seen only *when the person concerned turns round*. Dr Wiltse (p. 5) said, "*Looking back*, I saw a small cord like a spider's web", Muldoon (p. 18), "I managed to *turn around*. There was another 'me' lying quietly on the bed. My two identical bodies were joined by means of an elastic-like cable." William Gerhardi, M.A., B.LITT. (p. 29), out of his body, used the *observation* that the "cord" was *behind* his forward-moving Astral Body to prove to himself the reality of his experience. He asked, "How do I know I am not dreaming this?" and answered, "Look for the lighted cord *behind* you!" He looked, saw it, and was satisfied. Later (p. 31) Gerhardi said, "I wonder whether I may not have really died unawares? I ... *turned round*. But the silver cord, faint and thin, was still there." Wirt (p. 81) said, "I float out of, and away from, my fleshly form ... I now *look back* and see my body ... and further I see the silver cord or chain connecting my Spiritual (Astral or Soul) Body with the earthly body." Margaret Newby (p. 52) knew that she had *failed* to see her "silver cord" because she had *not* looked down from her released Astral Body on to her vacated physical body. These cases are chiefly British and American. Here is one from Norway. Ingeborg (Judge Dahl, *We are Here!*, Rider, p. 145) out of her body, observed a "cord" which "looked like gutta percha" and said "It is *following* me!"

The present writer has suggested that the formation of the "silver cord" roughly corresponds to what occurs when a child takes a piece of chewing-gum and pulls it out into two smaller pieces—so long as the process is not carried too far, a strand of gum subsists between them. In any case, those who would maintain that the "silver cord" is no more than a symbol or mental image, and not an objective extension of an objective Astral Body, are faced with an impossible task—that of providing a reasonable alternative explanation of the above (and other) facts.

If proof were needed of the fact that Muldoon made a contribution of the first importance to his subject, we have it in the fact that he was able to declare that the "experts" (Drs Lancelin, Carrington, etc.) had failed to record the existence and to insist on the importance of the "silver cord". He himself (op. cit., 1929, p. 29) provided much first-hand information on this important feature (which Staveley Bulford, *Man's Unknown Journey*, Rider, 1941, p. 133, described as "the missing link in psychical research").

Turning from astral projectors to a case of projection during hypnotic trance, Reine, the sensitive of P. E. Cornillier (op. cit., 1921), may be noted. She (p. 20), like several astral projectors, compared her "silver cord" to "*a ray of sunlight*" and (p. 151) variously described it as "a cord", "a fluidic cord", and (p. 395) "a fluidic line". Its function, she said, was to transmit vitality from the Astral Body to the physical body. When it snaps, the body dies (p. 207).

Mrs Keeler's "communicators" (p. 692) stated that the Astral Body does not, while the physical body does, cast "a shadow" in the Astral World, and (p. 708) that the "silver cord" "casts a shadow on the Astral Plane". These are interesting observations: they suggest that the "cord" is composite—that it consists of an extension both of the Astral Body and the physical body (or rather of its vehicle of vitality). This idea is supported by other "communicators" and is corroborated by actual observations. With regard to the former, two of Mrs M. E. Longley's "communicators" (*The Spirit World*, p. 156) stated that it included "an ethereal [= Astral] element" which, after its severance, was re-absorbed by *the Astral Body*. On the other hand, "Stead", communicating (*Life Eternal*, Wright & Brown, 1933, p. 79), said that after the "cord" snaps at death, part of it "falls back *into the physical body*". Another "communicator", that of S. Bedford (*Death—An Interesting Journey*, Alcuin Press, pp. 53, 114), in fact, combined these two statements when he said that the "cord" "partakes of two natures", while the "communicator" of *I Awoke* (David Stott, 1895, p. 23), years before the Keeler "communications" had been received, even more explicitly and significantly, said: "*The extension* of the [physical] body and *the extension* of the Astral Body form a chain which still unites the two."

These "communications" that support those received by Mrs Keeler are corroborated by observations made at deathbeds by Dr A. J. Davis in America and the Revd. William Stainton Moses in England. Davis (*Answers to Ever-Recurring Questions*, 1868), years before the Keeler "communications" had been received, described the Astral Body as related to the physical body by means of "vital electricity" and to the Spirit by "vital magnetism" and he described how he observed these two elements re-absorbed into the physical body and Astral Body respectively when the "cord" snapped at death.

(E) THE FREE "DOUBLE"—MENTAL FEATURES

1. THE APPEARANCE OF SPIRITS TO ASTRAL PROJECTORS

THE "COMMUNICATIONS": "Spirits, being in the Astral, of course have auras which, to a person developing, may appear as *small blue lights* until he actually enters one, when he sees *the person* [= Soul Body] to whom it belongs" (pp. 648, 658). Again, "The *aura* (or soul atmosphere) of a spirit is different from its *form. This aura, at a great distance, may appear like a small blue point, nearer, as a round blue object about a foot in diameter : when near enough to be seen distinctly as ... luminous mist about the size of a living being*" [= a *"column" or pillar of light*] (p. 698–9). Still again (p. 682): "The *eyes* are often the first part of a spirit to be seen by a person developing. The astral eyes of a person are about the only part of the Astral Body to be fully organized before development, and even then they are closed. They are situated back of the physical eyes." Finally (p. 698): "The fact that spirits are *first seen as transparent* is due to the defective vision which does not catch all the vibrations; *at a later stage [in development] the bodies appear quite solid.*"

Corroborations of "communications" by astral projectors, etc.

The fact that spirits may first appear to astral projectors as *"small blue lights"* (stated by Mrs Keeler's "communicators" in America) is supported by actual astral projectors in France, etc., by clairvoyants in England, etc.

Cornillier's sensitive Reine (op. cit., 1921, p. 20) first described *"a glimmering light"*, *"a luminous mist"*, and *"a kind of shining smoke"*. Cornillier (op. cit., p. 50) summed up Reine's observations thus: "When spirits are in the normal conditions of astral life, they have—at least for Reine in hypnosis—the aspect of glimmering lights ... But when they wish to manifest themselves to mortals, *they assume (in order to be recognized) the physical appearance* which was theirs on earth." Reine also (op. cit., p. 178), exactly like Mrs Keeler's "communicators", described seeing *"small blue lights"*: this, she said, was their "normal appearance" [i.e., when they did not need to "build-up" with ectoplasm for the purpose of recognition]. She tentatively used various other descriptive terms none of which, however, satisfied her—"*sparks*", "*flames*", "*phosphorescent clouds*" and "*tongues of fire*" (compare Acts 1, 2). On p. 130 it was said, "The general form of these lights seems to be *oblong*."

On one occasion, Reine (op. cit., pp. 63, 178) saw "*a blue light*" (which transformed itself into "a head and shoulders"), on another, "*a small blue light, a tongue of blue fire*". When another discarnate sould tried to show himself to Reine but failed, she said, "He is here, but I do not see him: I only feel his presence. He cannot manifest himself yet ... Wait ... *I see a sort of white cloud with two brilliant spots* [= *the eyes*]. He is doing all he can to make me see him ... No! He cannot!"

Clairvoyants give identical descriptions. Miss "Morton" (*Proc. S.P.R.*, viii, p. 311) saw a spirit "like *the flame of a candle*", and Grace Cooke (*Plumed Serpent*, Psychic Book Club, p. 58), "*a glowing ball of white light*". Mrs Leonard (*My Life in Two Worlds*, Cassell, 1931, p. 23) observed "*a circular patch of light*". She continued, "*In this light I saw my (newly-deceased) mother.*"

The "communicators" stated that "*the eyes*" were often the first part of a spirit to be seen by an astral projector. Professor F. W. Pawlowski of the University of Michigan gave the following description of a seance with Kluski (*Journ.* A.S.P.R., XX, 1926): "Bright *bluish stars* appear and begin to move ... near the ceiling. When they approach me at a distance of about sixteen inches, I recognized to my great astonishment that *they were human eyes* looking at me. Within a few seconds such a pair of eyes develops into *a complete human head* ... The eyes looked at me intently, the face smiled most pleasantly." Dr Nandor Fodor (*Encyclopedia of Psychic Science*, Arthurs Press, 1938, p. 208) stated, "The appearance of *psychic lights* usually heralds materialisations. *A disc of light* may transform itself into *a face*, *a star* into *a human eye*. To the touch, the 'light' is sometimes hard, sometimes sticky."

Just as Mrs Keeler's "communicators" described how what was first seen as "a small blue point" developed into a luminous mist about the size of a living person, i.e., a "column" or "pillar", J. V. H. (*Death's Door Ajar*, 1934, p. 78) observed that "lights" often appear on the heads of those present at seances. He said, "They may ultimately join together and create quite *a pillar of light*." Mrs Speers and others who were present at the seances

of the Revd. William Stainton Moses (*Spirit Teachings*, L.S.A.,
p. 14) observed (1) "*a pillar of light*" and (2) "*a cluster of lights* in
oblong shape" [Compare Reine]. "Imperator" stated that "the
pillar" was himself and the smaller "lights" were his helpers.

Wilfred Brandon (*Open the Door!*, Knopf, 1935, p. 155) made the
same observations in England as Mrs Keeler's "communicators"
in America. He stated, "Our friend who is strange to these things
sees at first only *lights* instead of people. There is such powerful
radio-activity in the Etheric Body that its rays quite blind one who
is not yet adjusted. Presently, he is able to discover, within the
flashing nimbus or aura, *a human being*."

2 CREATIVE ABILITIES

THE "COMMUNICATIONS": "In going out, one should have *an open
mind* [no specific expectations or preconceptions] as to what *the
experience* will be like and as to what he will *see*; otherwise his
prepossessions will tend to objectify themselves in thought-forms and he
will be unable to discriminate between them and the real objects
of the Astral World" (p. 684). "The *image* of a twirling *star
suspended in space* is sometimes used to promote the development
of astral hearing. Also the use of a cone of half-circles, diminishing
in diameter as they recede from the person" (p. 686). "The
attempt to visit the Himalayas in the *imagination* is used to stim-
ulate *motion* in the Astral Body, and it is said to be especially useful
[to Hall] because the oriental guides directing operations in the
writer's case had lived there, so that a certain rapport was established" (p. 687). "Concentration for a short time upon an actual
physical light may be used to help him keep a certain position
after he has risen to it. This is said to be not at all like the use of
light for hypnosis. He may also be told to concentrate on the
image of himself as *a point of light*; or upon yellowish-white points
of light in space" (p. 689).

Other mental images that were recommended were given above
(p. 3) in "*Techniques that facilitate the release and control of the
'double'*" and it was there noted that the "communicators" stated
that what we "*imagine*" is actually *created* in the Astral World.

They indicated a second outcome of our creative abilities when
they said, "Imagination is really the training of the higher (astral)
senses—hence the importance of *directing even casual thoughts*, as

they affect the Astral Body". (Hall cited the Bible as to our responsibility for every idle word or thought, i.e., Matt. xii, 36.)

A third outcome of our creativeness was indicated by the "communicators" in relation to *faith*. They said (p. 681) "Doubt hinders development because it prevents intense *imagination* [= *creation*] of the desired conditions, which tends to bring them about." Later (p. 706) he put the matter in a positive light: "Thought *creates* things; in that a person may help a thing to occur by believing it is likely to happen."

Corroboration of the "communications" by astral projectors, etc.

Muldoon (p. 212) found that "no two [astral projectors] have the same experience" and observed that the reason is that "the very things which are true on one occasion, *in one particular condition of mind*, would be entirely different on another occasion, when in *a different mental state*". He continued, "*It seems that the mind creates its own environment*—yet *the environment is real!*" He also echoed the idea given by the "communicators" as to the need to direct all our thoughts and actions, volitions and mental images— "even our casual thoughts", saying, "One must learn to will correctly ... your wrong thoughts create their own environment. This place ... is here ... in the earth's atmosphere ... the lower astral conditions. So far as higher astral conditions are concerned, I know nothing ... No one understands the astral world. It is too complicated. What holds true on one occasion is anything but true on another occasion."

A writer in *The London Forum* (March, 1935) made the discovery for himself that was "communicated" to Mrs Keeler and published in America in 1916. He observed: "Between Astral projection proper [= the projection of the Astral Body] and mind projection [= imagining that the Astral Body has projected] extend degrees of projection which may partake of the nature of both forms. Mental projection is the first step toward astral projection."

Muldoon (op. cit., 1936, p. 119) quoted "L.G.T." as observing, "I have noticed that when one is in the Astral, *thought becomes fact*, i.e., what I often see is really not there but seems to be *a materialization of thoughts* ..."

Oliver Fox (*Astral Projection*, Rider) made use of the creative abilities of the mind to produce projections of the Astral Body—

when out of his body and *dreaming*, i.e., unconsciously creating conditions in the "Astral", he noted incongruities between his created environment and the physical world (e.g., the paving-stones were differently aligned) and thus "awoke" from the dream into a true projection.

The difference between the subjective and the objective and the fact that "objective forms can be created by the power of thought" were discussed by Muldoon and Carrington in *The Phenomena of Astral Projection* (Rider, 1951, pp. 19–21).[1]

Yram (*Practical Astral Projection*, Rider, p. 137) said, "I have visited different dimensions, different planes ... *Each state of density*, or dimensional division of the ether, corresponds to *our affinities, desires and preferences.* Each one is therefore able to lead the life he *wishes.*"

In view of man's creative abilities (obvious in astral matter, obscure in physical matter), the further statement of Mrs Keeler's "communicators" that nothing is "small and unimportant"—that every thought and word and mental image has an effect, that life is "all one piece", is understandable.

The impact of these matters on "faith" is also clear: this important activity, like the "imagination", is often greatly misunderstood. Whereas it is often supposed to be self-deceit it is actually self-expression.

Horatio W. Dresser (*The Open Vision*, Harrap, p. 40) observed, "Experience with spontaneously-given 'communications' teaches that *the believing attitude* is the one into which the spirit must grow." Again (p. 60): "Quimby grew in intuitive discernment ... The first clue was the discovery of clairvoyance or intuition on his own part, and the fact that this power grew with *use*, i.e., by *depending on it* ..."

Sydney T. Klein (*The Way of Attainment*, Rider, 1924, p. 85) put this in religious terminology. He said, "Christ's teaching is very clear. 'All things whatsoever ye ask in prayer *believing*, ye shall receive. True prayer for spiritual gifts is based therefore on our inner consciousness, our realization of the presence of God *within* ..." Jesus (John vii, 38) declared: "Whoever *believes* in me, streams of living 'water' shall flow out from *within* him."

[1] The photograph they mention of Felicia Scatcherd, cannot, however, be found at the College of Psychic Science, S.W.7.

Arthur Ford (*Nothing So Strange*, Harper Bros., 1958, p. 21), the famous American psychic, said, "Because I am one who constantly works with ESP I *believe* there are no unsurmountable barriers between us and the answer to our needs. There is something about disbelief that blocks the reach of the mind ..."

Phoebe Payne, the equally famous English sensitive, gave the reason for the power both of faith and of unfaith, each to produce its characteristic results. In a book entitled *Man's Latent Powers* (Faber, 1938, p. 51) she pointed out that psychic abilities depend upon the activities of the sense organs of the Soul Body, the "chakras" of the Yogis. While, on the one hand, trust, assurance, confidence and tranquility, i.e., *faith*, facilitates their expansion and activity, on the other hand, dislike, distrust, doubt, fear, anxiety, etc., i.e., *unfaith*, contracts and therefore paralyses them.

Faith is not only of the first importance on the psychic and spiritual "levels" of man's total self: it is also of the first importance to his physical well-being. In a book entitled *The Will to Health*, published in 1961, Dr Harley Williams said, "If you have a strong religious belief, hold on to it and make it stronger. This kind of faith has preventive efficiency superior to drugs, vaccines and prophylactics."

Emotion is an element in faith. As early as the thirteenth century, Albertus Magnus regarded "an excess of emotion" as the basis of "magical influence". In 1961, Dr Louisa Rhine (*Hidden Chambers of the Mind*, Wm. Sloane Associates) told of a boy who, before being tested for psychical ability, was promised a highly desired toy as a reward for good results. His emotions were so aroused that he "trembled from head to toe". The results were excellent.

That faith has an *emotional* tone was observed by Professor Ian Stevenson, M.D., who (*Harpers*, July 1959) agrees with the findings of Drs Pratt and J. B. Rhine, as follows: "The novelty of tests of ESP stimulates many beginners to performances which are well above chance, but which they do not sustain after the initial *enthusiasm* wears off."

The Austrian Countess Nora Wydenbruck (*The Paranormal*, Rider & Co. Ltd., 1939, p. 150) said that St Thérèse of Lisieux "repeatedly saved her sisterhood from financial disaster by the prayers which she uttered with *complete and absolute faith*". She further observed (p. 145), "To my husband and myself this faith in a protective power brought about the cases of 'direct inter-vention' which we experienced—incidents slight in themselves, and yet undoubtedly belonging to the category of miracles."

The prayer of *absolute faith* has been observed, in many coun-tries and at various times, to produce surprising results. In Ger-many Augustus Hermann Francke (1663–1727), impressed with the needs of destitute children, organized an orphanage: he fed and educated between 2,000 and 3,000 children purely by prayer with faith. Samuel Jackson, in his biography of the German physician Jung Stilling (1740–1817) recorded the fact that his edu-cation was obtained by a succession of "miracles" in answer to fervent prayer. Jean Baptiste Vianney, the Curé d'Ars (1786–1859) did the same in France as Francke did in Germany, while George Müller did the same in Bristol. The last-mentioned wrote a book entitled *The Life of Trust.*

Writing in *Light* (LXXVII, 1957, p. 53), Dr L. J. Bendit, M.D., discussed the de la Warr camera, the Abrams box, pendulum, divining-rods, etc. and observed, "(a) only certain people are capable of detecting either disease, water or minerals and (b) they have to *believe* that the apparatus they are using is effective".

In America one of our greatest clairvoyants, Mrs Eileen J. Garrett (*Telepathy*, Creative Age Press Inc., 1941), made many references to the importance of faith in the successful conduct of experiments in telepathy. On p. 46 of that book she stated: "I per-ceive because of both *a belief that I can know* and that I desire to know." On p. 62 she gave the *modus operandi* as follows: "When the experiment is to be telepathic, there is one very important point to remember. Any slight suggestive image must be noticed and *accepted on faith* and put down for what it is—not interpreted by mental association. *The great obstacle to getting telepathic images is lack of faith in what appears.*" She concluded: "The tendency is to think, 'Oh, that's nothing! Why doesn't something important come?'"

In Great Britain Professor H. H. Price (*Light*, LXXX, 1960, p. 59) said that when one writes a book, "The *creative* part of the work is done outside consciousness"—one must wait for ideas to come—it is "inspiration". After the ideas do come, conscious work, that of selecting, etc., is necessary. He pointed out that the process can be facilitated as follows: (1) Before going to sleep, make a brief review of the main points of the subject. (2) Suggest to yourself that at (say) 10 a.m. the next day the desired thoughts will occur to you. (3) At 10 a.m. be seated with pencil and paper. "*At the time of making the suggestion to yourself, a certain tranquil confidence is needed (faith, if you like)*". On the other hand, "Anxiety and fussiness are likely to have an inhibiting effect."

In America, Dr Gertrude Schmeidler conducted experiments in E.S.P. (ESP in Relation to Rorschacht Test Evaluation, Parapsychological Monographs, No. 2, 1960) and found that "*believers*" are likely to show higher scores than "doubters": with a "working hypothesis" that almost everyone has some psychic ability, she concluded that the "doubters" suffer from "an unconscious negativism".

In Czechoslovakia, Dr Milan Rýzl (*Journ.* S.P.R., 41, 1962, p. 240) experimented with psychic abilities under hypnosis. He found it necessary to convince the subject "that he is *able to* acquire the ability of ESP—that he *will* acquire it". Rýzl (p. 245) several times observed that the persons who possessed a well-trained ESP lost it after a time and he concluded that they still had the ability but that its action was *inhibited* by "a *dislike* of further experiments".

The negative aspect of faith has been mentioned incidentally above: it needs to be stressed almost as much as the positive aspect. Dr Gardner Murphy, the distinguished American psychologist, recently published a book entitled *The Challenge of Psychical Research* (Hamish Hamilton, 1962). In it he asked why the great mediums of the past (Mrs Piper, Mrs Leonard, etc.) have not been replaced by equally great ones? He said, "Perhaps we have here a circular relationship: doubt inhibiting the development of mediumship and the failure of mediumship adding to doubt."

3. MORAL AND SPIRITUAL CONSIDERATIONS

THE "COMMUNICATIONS": "A pure and noble person has an Astral Body which is much finer in matter than one who is more 'earthy'. One can change the Astral Body and refine it by an ethical life and, to some extent, by a certain diet" (p. 642). "If one lives an ethical life one rises to a comparatively advanced position after death" (p. 644). "Ethical conduct helps because it produces harmony, poise and the all-round development of the Astral Body, and helps to carry a person calmly through the final sudden separation of the two bodies, so that the person on awaking in the Astral World is not confused" (p. 660).

Corroboration of the "communications" by astral projectors, etc.

In France, Reine (op. cit., 1921, p. 35) observed that "The facility in disengaging [from the physical body] ... would seem to be in direct proportion to the [ethical and spiritual] evolution." It is "the privilege of a spirit that has already attained a high degree of evolution" (p. 387). Again, "Spirits who have reached a high degree of evolution are able to disengage themselves during sleep and go to consult with the superior spirits" (p. 186). "The possibility of freeing oneself bears a relation to one's evolution and you certainly gain much in this way, since you learn to comprehend many things which, when you are awake, in normal life [back in the physical body], become *intuitions*" (p. 309).

In America, Muldoon (op. cit., p. 72) gave techniques for the production of projections. He also said, "A word of warning! If you are nervous, easily influenced, lacking in 'will', fearful, if you live in an atmosphere of discord, do *not* try to practice astral projection; turn towards physical culture rather than psychical culture."

In France, Yram (*Practical Astral Projection*, Rider, p. 26), like Mrs Keeler's "communicators", said that the essential conditions for satisfactory projection include the following. (1) physical health, serenity, moderation in food-intake and the absence of "highly alcoholic drinks". (2) "It is essential to realize the seriousness of the undertaking". "A peaceful life is necessary" and prayer and meditation help by affecting our thoughts, desires and motives. He continued, "The shortest way is to choose a noble ideal and to make it the essential point round which will shine all thoughts, desires and motives for action. *This noble idea must be your goal—for this alone you should work*." (3) The psychic faculties demand "the power to concentrate one's thoughts on a single subject, ... the practice of rhythmic breathing, relaxation, and finally, the ability to suspend thought completely".

What are the reasons for these injunctions? (1) One who over-eats will never project the Astral Body; one who takes alcohol in excess may project but, if he does (or rather, whether he does or not) he will attract undesirables. (2) One who neglects to cultivate (and live for) a noble ideal automatically attracts undesirables and his "last state will be worse than his first"—they will lead him to disaster. (3) Those who neglect psychical development may project the Astral Body but the Astral Body will not be under control and the observations that are made through it will sometimes be unsatisfactory and misleading.

Yram (p. 76) said exactly the same as Mrs Keeler's "communicators"—"The double is the more tied to the physical body the more crude (or material) its composition." Reine (op. cit., p. 387) said this in converse—that the ability of a "double" to leave a body is "the privilege of a person who has already attained a high degree of [moral and spiritual] evolution", i.e., of a person whose double is relatively refined and subtle, corresponding to his thoughts, wishes and intentions.

Yram (p. 92) gave an illustration of the generalization "communicated" through Mrs Keeler regarding the importance of our thoughts, even the casual ones. When out of his body, Yram spoke "an unfortunate phrase": he said, "I had barely finished speaking, when I fêlt a shock, followed by a giddy descent which brought me back into my body." He considered the experience and concluded, "I understood that *each thought is, in itself, a vibratory world* in the selection of which greater care must be taken the further one goes from earth conditions. Images and ideas sent forth by thought must always express some [good and positive] quality, never a fault. All ideas of money, vanity, egotism, evil, hatred, etc., must go." He concluded, "*Remember these conditions— they are indispensable in the higher regions!*" (It must be obvious that they are of the first importance in all regions, including the physical conditions of earth-life—they need to be stated and their indispensability emphasized only because mortals are usually blind to the fact: our awareness is limited; we fail to see that greed, vanity, egotism, evil thoughts, etc., always and inevitably produce evil results in our minds and environments; once we are free from the "blinkers"-like body, the fact is apparent).

Yram observed, "The experience of projections in the different dimensions ['spheres', 'planes', 'conditions', 'environments', etc.] of space allows us to infer, with absolute certainty, the existence of *an order of Principles in action throughout the Universe.*"

He summed up the desirable moral and spiritual attitude as follows. "Whatever the kind of attraction which is affecting us, *we* must never act towards it in a negative manner ... If it is personal, depreciating and hostile, *we* must remove its negative character—then this impulse will become our servant. *Our consciousness must be centred fully on the Good, the Beautiful and the True.*"

In South Africa, Professor J. H. M. Whiteman (*The Mystical Life*, Faber, 1961, p. 20) said much the same as Yram (and Mrs Keeler's "communicators"). On p. 51 he also confirmed, from his own experiences of projection, what the "communicators" said regarding the vitalising effect of projections that are of natural origin. He said, "If separation [= projection] proceeds as the result of *a balanced and rational development of character* [and not from shock, physical weakness, drugs, etc.], it has, in my experience, no different effect on the physical body from that of *a deep and refreshing sleep.*" He noted that various kinds of fixation affect the projected person: (a) intellectual fixations (e.g., fixed ideas, hasty assumptions, wishful thinking); (b) emotional fixations (e.g., ambitions) and (c) sensory fixations. Since he was seeking the ideals mentioned by Yram, even though he was "caught up in conflict" for "a few moments" during one projection, he rose above "the levels of fantasy-influence" [= above the vehicle of vitality and the corresponding "Hades" conditions into the unenshrouded Soul Body and "Paradise" conditions]. He later returned to his physical body "with all strain vanished and with a new and zestful outlook on physical life".

On p. 58 Dr Whiteman gave an actual example of the creative effect of thoughts [which is visible during projections], and on p. 59 commented *"that the moral side of life cannot be divorced from the intellectual side is shown in such experiences as this ..."*. He had been obliged first to reject fixed ideas, then a tendency to judge by appearances—"in short, fixation of every kind". He held, *"Fixation of every kind is at once anti-intellectual (in blinding our perceptions) and anti-moral (in acting contrary to the Good)".*

Dr Whiteman (p. 55) found that the "psychical states" or "levels" of consciousness that he reached during his "separations", i.e., astral projections, were "far more real than physical states—as if one had for the first time become really awake". Nevertheless he also enjoyed "mystical states" which were still more "real". Like all mystics, he found that physical objects (including our physical bodies) are relatively "unreal": that what is enduring in earth-life are our moral and spiritual activities.

Mrs Keeler's "communicators" (p. 654) stated that a trained astral projector gets "into touch with advanced spirits" and learns from them (and has the opportunity of fuller life and helpfulness). They said (p. 659), "Development (of astral projection) has *a social aspect* and it may happen that a person is able to see more *as a means to help someone else* than he can for his own progress merely."

The present writer has met a number of people who, having had astral projections, were inordinately proud of the fact: they felt different from, indeed superior to, people who have not had (or rather have not *remembered* having had) them. They regarded astral projections as an end in themselves. But, like all our "gifts", they have moral and spiritual implications and, if not used in that context, will mislead rather than help. "The fruit of the *spirit*", said St Paul (Gal. v, 22), "is love, joy, peace, longsuffering, gentleness, goodness, faith." No psychic abilities, or intellectual powers, were mentioned. It is possible, in satisfactory projections, to receive teaching and help from advanced discarnate sources and, although this may not be specifically remembered, it forms the basis of inspiration and intuition. It is also possible to help others while projected, to help sick mortals, the dying, the newly-dead and the earthbound—see the writer's book *During Sleep*—the possibility of "co-operation" (Theosophical Publishing House, 1964).

(F) THE FREE *"DOUBLE"*—BODILY FEATURES

1. A FORWARD-MOVING "DOUBLE" MAY LEAVE A TRAIL OF "LIGHT"

THE "COMMUNICATIONS": "As the Astral Body moves, it leaves *a trail of light*" (p. 646). "Spirits in motion leave *a trail of light* from the motion of their Astral Bodies" (p. 689).

Corroboration of the "communications" by astral projectors, etc.

In France, Yram (p. 62) stated, "Several times I have noticed *a white luminous cloud* trailing my double." On p. 66 he said, "During this experience I noticed *a phosphorescent streak* left in the wake of my body."

In America, Muldoon (p. 13) stated, "Streaks of *light* (scintillations) are thrown off by the Astral Body and extend backward about two feet as it moves along at this speed (intermediate between that of walking and supernormal movement)." Again (p. 93), "One can observe this *neuric energy* ..., luminous, like white light ... It is the scintillations of this energy which trail along behind the phantom [= Astral Body] when the latter is moving at the intermediate speed."

We suggest that this "trail of light", described by Mrs Keeler's "communicators" in 1916 and actually observed by Yram and Muldoon, has often been seen in relation to the moving Astral Bodies of both the "dead" and the living and that it was this observation, and not pure fantasy, that gave rise to the idea that angels "fly" by means of "wings".

2. THE RELEASED "DOUBLE" ACTS LIKE A CONDENSER OF COSMIC VITALITY

THE "COMMUNICATIONS": "The purpose of sleep is to renew the Astral Body. During sleep, the vibrations [= vehicle of vitality] holding down the Astral Body to the physical body are partly relaxed, and *the Astral Body sometimes gets a little way outside of the physical and above it*. The first *complete* going out may be *in sleep*. As development (of astral projection) progresses, *a person needs less*

sleep, as the Astral Body is out more and gets refreshed without it"
(p. 696).

Corroborations of the "communications" by astral projectors, etc.

Muldoon (op. cit., p. 68) said the same. "Every time you sleep your Astral Body moves slightly out of coincidence—perhaps only a fraction of an inch, perhaps more. This discoincidence [of *the vehicle of vitality*] has little to do with one's ability to project [the *Astral Body*] even though projection is an extension of discoincidence. One can be ... entirely immune to astral projection, yet his Astral Body always slightly discoincides during sleep."

Reine (op. cit., 1921, pp. 386–7, 589) said exactly the same. "What causes sleep is a disunion between the Astral Body and the physical body. The purpose of this disunion is to liberate sufficiently the Astral Body so that it may go to gather from the ambience the vital force contained in its magnetic and cosmic currents whose emission or passage is intensified and facilitated by the night. In this way the stock of force that is spent in daily activity is constantly renewed. The amount supplied by the physical body by means of food, respiration, etc., could not suffice to sustain life if the breath of the vital, cosmic force did not come to fortify it. This is a universal law, governing all living creatures.

"This sortie of the Astral Body for the purpose of gathering nourishment is not to be confounded with the disengagement of highly-evolved persons in quest of information or influences that may develop their consciousness. The first [involving the disengagement of the *vehicle of vitality*] is common to ... everything that lives [plants and animals as well as man]. The second [involving the disengagement of the *Astral Body*] is the privilege of a man who has already attained a high degree of [mental, moral and spiritual] evolution."

Muldoon (p. 68) quoted Carrington as follows: "We shall never arrive at a satisfactory theory of sleep, doubtless, until we admit the presence of a vital force and the existence of an individual human spirit which withdraws more or less completely from the body during the hours of sleep and derives spiritual invigoration and nourishment during its sojourn in the spiritual world." Carrington referred to his book entitled *Vitality, Fasting and Nutrition* (pp. 225–350), to *Journ. A.S.P.R.*, April 1908 and *Our*

Psychic Science, August 1908, where he advanced the theory that the human body more nearly resembles the electric motor than it does the steam-engine.

Dr Wm. Wilson (*After Life*, Rider, p. 82) said, "Sleep is not due to physiological brain-changes, but *the withdrawal of the 'soul' from the everyday world. In this way it seeks communion with the primordial rhythm of life*." The Yogis have, of course, said this sort of thing for thousands of years.

Mrs Eileen J. Garrett (*My Life as a Search for the Meaning of Mediumship*, Rider, 1939, p. 5), having described her childhood experiences, said, "The air around sustained and fed me as though I had received food and drink." Later (p. 30) she said, "I observed how the living trees and flowers drew their air and colour from the dancing globules of light which filled what people know as space. Such globules I had first seen, long before, in my room and I knew that the entire atmosphere was made up of these little dancing balls of light ... *I knew that the night air, whatever it contained, charged and re-charged all living things with new and strange vitality ... I watched the plants and flowers feed themselves upon this strange night-force ...*"

3. THE RANGE OF ASTRAL TRAVEL

THE "COMMUNICATIONS": "There is apparently no difficulty to the trained person in going anywhere he desires. Thus, mere concentration on a place takes him there. (The same is true of spirits who come to visit mortals.)" (p. 698).

Corroboration of the "communications" by astral projectors, etc.

Many of the astral projectors whose testimonies were cited and analysed in *The Study and Practice of Astral Projection* made this personal observation. This applied, for example, to Geddes' doctor friend (p. 58), Dr Ostby (p. 88), etc.

(G) THE RETURN OF THE "DOUBLE" TO THE PHYSICAL BODY

THE "COMMUNICATIONS": This causes a "blackout" of consciousness (see p. 37).

Corroboration of the "communications" by astral projectors, etc.

A number of projectors experienced a "blackout" when they re-entered their bodies (*see* p. 7).

HALL'S OWN OBSERVATIONS

As already said, the present writer did not see *Journ.* A.S.P.R., XII, 1918 (containing Prescott Hall's article entitled "Experiments in Astral Projection"[1]) until 12 August, 1963, i.e., after the above had been written.

Over a period of six years, Hall tried the techniques that had been "communicated" to him *via* Mrs Keeler. But he remained "still in doubt" as to whether astral projection is a fact or not. The "communicators" told him that his Astral Body was very strongly attached to his physical body and he said this was possible, since, on the one hand, his relatives had all died late in life and, on the other hand, it required more than twice the usual amount of ether or nitrous oxide to render him unconscious (which is presumably a good index to the matter).

In his "Summary and Conclusions" (p. 56) Hall stated: "*Supernormal sight and hearing* were what the writer was trying for;

---

[1] Hall warned his readers that the exercises, etc., that he had received in the Keeler "communications" should not be undertaken without expert guidance. That warning applies to all attempts at psychic development and particularly to Yoga breathing exercises. The study of psychic experiences and their implications is of great value: any attempt to force them may be definitely dangerous to health. Over a century ago (1848) Mrs Catherine Crowe wrote: "By annihilating the necessities of the body, we may loosen the bonds of the Spirit [Astral or Soul Body] and enable it to manifest some of its inherent endowments [clairvoyance, telepathy, foreknowledge, etc.]. Ascetics and saints have frequently done this voluntarily, and disease or a peculiar constitution [= a "loose" vehicle of vitality] sometimes do it for us involuntarily. While it is undesirable that we should seek to produce such a state, it is extremely desirable that we should avail ourselves of the instruction to be gained by the knowledge that such phenomena exist and that thereby our connexion with the Spiritual World may become a demonstrated fact."

all that he got, such as it was, concerned these two senses." But he could not decide whether they were supernormal or not. He said, "The most definite objects seen were: (a) A Greek profile and the head and shoulders of a Hindu in a turban; (b) the brilliant red object; (c) large round blue lights; (d) small round blue or yellow lights; (e) landscapes ...; (f) patches of mist or colour, frequently about the size of persons, but showing no definite details ..."

He also mentioned "two sorts of things, of which it is difficult to say whether they were seen or felt"—chiefly "figures, definitely of persons ... surrounded by other objects like trees or *columns* ...". A number of "sounds" were also heard.

Later (p. 49) Hall, in America, made a highly significant observation: he said that he saw, "One bright light and many small blue ones." We suggest that the "bright [?white] light" was the form of his chief teacher, while the "many small blue ones" were those of his assistants. As already said (p. 57), those present at a seance of the Revd. William Stainton Moses (*Spirit Teachings*, Fowler, p. 14), in England, made an identical observation. Reine, the sensitive of P. E. Cornillier in France (op. cit., 1921, p. 130), described the advanced spirits of the calibre of "Imperator" as "white, shining, golden-white" while their helpers were "a special blue—pure azure, luminous, intense" (op. cit., p. 60); one (p. 70) was "*a tongue of blue fire*" (compare Acts ii, 2).

In addition to definite sights—the profile of the Greek and the head of the Hindu—Hall reported what are called "spirit lights", i.e., imperfectly-seen spirits; he reported "small *blue* lights" (Vol. XII, 1918, pp. 47, 48), "one *bright* light [? a teacher] and many small ones" [? his assistants] (p. 49); "*lambent tongues of white light*" (p. 50)—compare Acts ii, 2; and "suggestions of eyes" (p. 51).

Hall stated that, although these experiences had not caused him to believe in "immortality", the success he achieved in eventually feeling free from his body made him "more disposed to grant the possibility of the Spiritualistic point of view" [i.e., of survival and occasional communication]. He insisted, "If nothing else is proved by such things, at best it is shown that the ordinary type of consciousness can be transcended."

Before his "Summary and Conclusions", Hall had given twelve

pages of text as "The Record" and this includes matters the significance of which had escaped him.

Moreover, Hall failed to realize the true nature of his quest, which was to duplicate the release of the Astral *Body*—if he had satisfactory evidence of *supernormal sight and hearing* that would not be demonstrated, since those phenomena might be due not to the release of the Astral *Body* but to clairvoyance and clairaudience (as, indeed, the "communicators"—Vol. X, 1916, p. 643—seem to have pointed out[1]). This matter was discussed in some detail by the writer in *The Study and Practice of Astral Projection*, 1961, p. 143.

Apart from this failure, Hall failed to observe several things in the "communications" that did suggest the projection of the Astral Body (necessarily, since, in the first place, he had not himself achieved more than the early stages of the release of his Astral *Body*—he was not a suitable subject, and, secondly, he had not at

---

[1] Additional techniques from "communicators", given in *Journ.* A.S.P.R., XII, 1918, pp. 44–55, by Prescott Hall, are as follows.

1. "Instruction to concentrate a yard or two in front of my body and to try and get towards that place."
2. "Instructions to concentrate on a spot above my head, instead of in front, and to try and rise from my body."
3. "Instructions to concentrate one foot seven inches above my head."
4. "Instructions to imagine breathing through my ears and to tell about, from time to time, what I see."
5. "Instructions to sit erect, not touching the chairback, and to concentrate on a *horizontal* bar above the line of sight; to *hold* breath when there is a feeling of *rising*; but in general to be more passive and to let the spirits (= 'deliverers') do the work."
6. "Instructions to brace hands and feet and contract muscles of stomach in order to force the Astral Body out; and to imagine the physical body *falling*."
7. "Instructions to imagine ascending a flight of steps which tip toward me, then to take hold of a silk rope and jump off, kicking the steps away, and *filling* the lungs at the same time."
8. "Instructions to try moving forward *horizontally* in a straight line."
9. "Instructions to imagine revolving rapidly on tiptoe, finally springing up."
10. "Instructions to imagine a disc three inches in diameter revolving rapidly seven inches in front of eyes."
11. "Instructions to imagine sitting in a swing with long ropes, swinging back and forth and sending impulses in the same direction as the swing at the end of each swing."
12. "Instructions to fly slowly and evenly in any direction."
13. "Instructions to be a soap-bubble, blown in any direction."
14. "Instructions to go to the Himalayas through the air."
15. "Instructions to imagine a point two feet in front of my throat, and to see it coming towards me until I merge with it and become a point."

his disposal testimonies of numerous people who have claimed to release their Astral Bodies).

We have indicated above a number of matters, given in the "communications", that were subsequently corroborated by astral projectors who had never heard of, much less read, Prescott Hall's records published in *Journ*. A.S.P.R., Vol. X, 1916.

On August 31st, 1909, Hall noted[1] "Freer from the body than before and able to move through it, especially *horizontally*." This experience followed an instruction, given by the "communicators" on August 19th, to "concentrate on a *horizontal* bar above the line of sight ...". It suggests an early stage in the projection of the Astral *Body*: it was indeed described by Muldoon as the first stage in his first projection (at the age of twelve years). Later, Muldoon's Astral Body became erect (a position not described by Hall).

On September 3rd, 1909, Hall reported: "Sense of physical body *falling* down and away. *Definite feeling that I am not in my body*. Faint music". The "communicators" took advantage of this observation and, on September 9th, recommended the technique numbered (6) in our footnote, p. 46. This sensation of falling is reported by a number of projectors as experienced when the Astral *Body* is released (See e.g., Muldoon, op. cit., 1929, pp. 41, 46, Leaf, cited in *The Study and Practice of Astral Projection*, 1961, p. 61, Lind, ibid., p. 68, etc.). Other projectors reported a sensation of *rising* (as did Hall on some occasions): the two are complementary —if consciousness is mainly centred in the physical body (and Hall's physical body was particularly strong) separation is felt as *falling*; if, on the other hand, it is mainly centred in the Astral Body it is felt as *rising* (see, for examples of projectors who reported this, *The Study and Practice of Astral Projection*, 1961, Miss Peters, p. 48, Miss Johnson, p. 54, Sigrid Kaeyer, pp. 57, 58, Hives, p. 59, Leaf, p. 61, Lind, pp. 68, 69, Mrs Boorman, p. 71, "N.D.", p. 104, etc.). These *sensations of falling or of rising*, observed by Hall and followed by "*a definite* feeling" of being out of the physical body, unrealized by him were indications of the projection of the Astral *Body*.

On October 7th, 8th and 10th Hall felt the efforts of "*deliverers*" —"feeling of being drawn out of the body ... Feeling of being pulled about". Many projectors report similar assistance.

On March 13th, 1910 he reported another experience that people have since often described in connexion with the release of the Astral *Body*. He had a *"sinking"* feeling (comparable to the sensation of *falling*, already noted), and said this was "followed by *a snap*, then a great yellowish light above me ... A new musical note ...". This "snap" or "click" was reported by numerous people who claimed to have released their Astral *Bodies*. Oliver Fox (*Astral Projection*, Rider, p. 56) said, "Once the little door had *clicked* behind, I enjoyed a mental clarity far surpassing that of earth life." Muldoon (op. cit., 1937, pp. 70, 158, 161, 162) recorded several cases—*"a snapping pain"*, *"a click"*, *"a crack"*, etc., and mentioned his earlier work (1929) in which he spoke of "A peculiar noise which seems close to the ear and inside the head ... a 'pop', 'sizz', etc. *This sound is usually heard just at the take-off of projection, as well as at the moment of coincidence,* and seems to be in the head ...". Mrs Piper described this phenomenon on return from trance (*Proc.* S.P.R., 28, 1915, p. 23).

On August 19th, 1910 Hall reported: "Body feels below me in space, and as if I were free from it, except at the base of the brain [where the 'silver cord' was attached?]. Distinct feeling of motion", while on November 29th he said, "I seemed to be able to look down on my own body, being rather surprised to see how bald the top of my head was."

We have seen that, in addition to the (admittedly small) amount of evidence that Hall recognized in his own experiences as supporting the theory of the projection of the Astral *Body*, there were details the value of which he overlooked.

CONCLUSIONS

Hall was "thoroughly sceptical" about these important things; Mrs Keeler neither knew nor cared about them. The conclusion seems unavoidable that the "communicators" knew more concerning them than Hall or Mrs Keeler; this is not particularly remarkable, but they also knew more than the experts on the subject, namely, Dr Lancelin in France and Dr Carrington in America—indeed, so far as we have information, they knew much more than any living person! Muldoon, who was to become justly famed for his numerous projections and the skill with which he observed them, advanced from 7 to 13 years of age while the "communications" were being received (unknown to him, of course).

Dr Hyslop, formerly Professor of Logic at Columbia University, New York (1916, p. 634), said, "The real problem in such material is first the purely psychological one, namely, to account for *the rich and versatile flow of ideas.*" He continued, "The product is not the result of careful education and study on the part of Mrs Keeler. *The very fertility of the ideas is sufficient to protect her against the suspicion of reproducing information that might come from ordinary reading.*" There was nothing that suggested "*personal beliefs and edited data*".

In addition to this, the "communicators" revealed many details that combine to form a coherent and logical whole and have since received corroboration (see Appendix I).

Hall (1918, p. 43) was trying to determine the relationship between "*a certain kind of exercise* and *certain observed results*" in his own experiments. He described various "colours" that he had "seen" and said, in a footnote, "The sketches in C. W. Leadbeater's *Man Visible and Invisible* (T.P.S., 1907) may help to give the reader some idea of this colour business. But, in many cases, the colours are far more brilliant than can be given by pigments. Arnold Bennett, when writing *The Glimpse* (Chapman and Hall, 2nd ed., 1909), must have seen or read about something of this kind." This comment of Prescott Hall's is also significant, for, according to a letter from Bennett to his sister, published in *Arnold Bennett, a Biography*, by Reginald Pound (Wm. Heinemann Ltd., 1952), Bennett's description was "taken bodily" from Dr Annie Besant's books on Theosophy!

Both Bishop Leadbeater's excellent book and Bennett's transcription of Theosophical teachings pre-dated the publication of the "communications" which (as Hall pointed out) they so closely resemble. As Dr James Hyslop said (1916, p. 635), Dr Besant, Leadbeater, etc., do not confirm the Keeler "communications"—"It is rather the reverse. If any importance be attached to the present records ['communications'], it must be on the ground that they help to determine what is possible in statements elsewhere [Theosophy, Rosicrucianism, Anthroposophy, etc.] which do not have credentials that would satisfy the scientific man."

The "communications" received by Hall weekly from 1909 to 1915, published in *Journ. A.S.P.R.*, X, 1916 (pp. 637–60, 679–

708), were partially misunderstood and, in any case, passed into oblivion. Although his experiments, based upon the techniques advised by the "communicators", fell short of anything definite, Hall achieved a greater confirmation of the reality of astral projection than he realized (*Journ.* A.S.P.R., XII, 1918, p. 39). His success was, indeed, beyond his deserts for the "communicators" recommended certain rules of life (abstinence from tobacco, alcohol, etc.), in addition to the exercises or techniques, and Hall neglected faithfully to observe these. He admitted (XII, 1918, p. 41) that this failure might account for the poverty of his results. He considered that these rules of life were "probably *based on experience*". Since they were given by "communicators", it is pertinent to ask, "*Whose* experience?" If the experience of a "subconscious" fragment of the mind of an unlettered woman can yield results beyond the knowledge of our most eminent psychologists, then the supposed "sub-conscious" fragments of the minds of quite ordinary folk are at a premium and the carefully-trained conscious minds of the psychologists who study them in numerous ingenious ways are at a discount: the "part", in fact, is much greater than the "whole".

The "communications" are amply corroborated, not on the grounds envisaged by Hall, namely, the use of the techniques provided in them, but by a critical analysis of the data that were not available to him, namely, the testimonies of numerous astral projectors who (1) had never heard of the "communications" and (2) had not used any experimental techniques whatever but whose Astral Bodies had been released in either a natural or an enforced manner, processes which produced results with significant differences. The latter were published by the present writer (The Study and Practice of Astral Projection, Aquarian Press, 1961).

It is now, we maintain, a reasonably-established fact that we possess a second, *objective*, four-dimensional body, popularly called the Astral or Soul Body (the "spiritual body" of St Paul, I Cor. xv, 35, 44), that may be released from our physical body temporarily during our physical embodiment—*and therefore presumably permanently when, eventually, the physical body is discarded. We survive death in the Astral or Soul Body.*

In Appendix I we tabulate a number of the details that have been brought to light in the present study: of the twenty items there listed, no less than thirteen (marked with an asterisk) were not (so far as we are aware) specifically mentioned either by the experts in astral projection (Dr Lancelin in France and Dr Carrington in U.S.A.), or the teachers who gave us the remarkably concordant philosophies known as Theosophy (Mme. Blavatsky, Dr Annie Besant, Bishop C. W. Leadbeater, etc.), Rosicrucianism (with three separate Schools, the Hermetic Order of the Golden Dawn, AMORC, and Max Heindel's Rosicrucian Fellowship), Anthroposophy (Dr Rudolf Steiner), etc. It is only fair to observe that these thirteen details were not, in fact, necessary to the purposes of these teachers, though we have found them to be of value in the vindication of certain of the fundamental doctrines which they gave out.

In the whole of the circumstances, it is incredible that the "communicators" who provided Hall with these techniques (which, as Dr Hyslop surmised, might eventually afford some confirmation to the basic teachings of Theosophy, etc.) were merely "subconscious" fragments of the unlettered, and actually quite uninterested, Mrs Keeler. The "communications" contain nothing in the nature of impersonation (in the sense of assuming characteristics and idiosyncracies which might belong to someone else) or dramatization. We do not doubt that they were the discarnate "orientals" that they claimed to be.

The details brought to light are not anti-Christian, anti-Buddhist, anti-Hindu or anti-Mohammedan; they are not primarily of religious significance[1] but are of psychological import. The dénouement has come after fifty years. As Longfellow said, "All things come round to him who will but wait!" The truth has proved "strange—stranger than fiction".

"If the revelations of the mystics really contain no unconscious reminiscences of what they have read, we find in them so many

---

[1] Although some psychic phenomena are obviously quite distinct from spiritual matters (and that applies particularly to "physical" phenomena), positive forms of psychism (including astral projections) are related to the moral and spiritual development of the person concerned. Ethical conduct, etc. refines the Astral or Soul Body, facilitating its temporary release, and renders the "silver cord"-extension highly elastic, facilitating independent travel (XII, 1918, pp. 45; X, 1916, p. 684 respectively). Jesus (John vii, 38) said, "Whoever believes in me, as the Scripture says (Isa. xii, 3), *streams of living water shall flow out from within him.*" Hall (XII, 1918, p. 48), clearly without realizing the possible significance of his observation (though made on a lower "level"), reported the following phenomena in his own case: "*Body blazing with streamers pouring in and out from solar plexus.*" Cases in which saints have been luminous are well-attested.

analogies with the teaching, which later became esoteric, of the great primitive religions, that we should be compelled to believe that ... this teaching exists, identical, latent and unchangeable, *corresponding with some objective and universal truth.*"—Maurice Maeterlinck, 1922.

APPENDICES

APPENDIX I

SUMMARIZING RESULTS OF THIS STUDY

Details given by "Communicators", 1909–15, *published in* 1916 (*J.A.S.P.R.*) *as to how Astral Projections may be Produced.*	Corroborative Details *given in Testimonies of* Astral Projectors (*unaware of the* "*Communications*")
1. Mortals possess a *vehicle of vitality* and *an Astral or Soul Body*, in addition to the dense physical body, and certain techniques favour their release to form a duplicate ("double") of the physical body.	1. Muldoon (1929), pp. 27, 167, 212; Yram, p. 137; Cornillier, pp. 3, 5, 45, 48, 88; Garrett (1941), pp. 40, 51, 59–60, 103, 104, 128–9, 193, (1943) pp. 17, 45, 90, 92, 116, 135, 138, (1949) pp. 7, 143, 164, 165; Crookall (1916) p. 187.
2. Some "doubles" are simple (consisting of *either* vehicle of vitality *or* Astral Body only); others are composite (Astral Body *plus* part or all of the vehicle of vitality).*	2. (a) Simple (vehicle of vitality only), Crookall (1961) pp. 31, 104; (b) simple (Astral Body only), Crookall (1961), pp. 37, 40, 88, etc.; (c) composite, ibid. pp. 3, 41, etc.
3. "Doubles" released in a *natural* manner show differences from those where release is *enforced*.*	3. Crookall, (1961) pp. 1411–43.
4. "Doubles" tend to be partly released in severe illness.	4. Muldoon (1929), pp. 14-15; Crookall (1961), pp. 3–20.
5. "Doubles" tend to be released in proportion as one is morally and spiritually developed.*	5. Muldoon (1929), pp. 72, 76, 92; Yram, p. 26; Cornillier (1921), p. 387; Whiteman (1961), pp. 20, 55, 58, 59.
6. Crossed hands and feet may hinder releases of "doubles".*	6. Cornillier (1921), pp. 122, 179, 288, 387; Crookall (1961), p. 162.
7. The separation of the "double" from the body causes a "*blackout*" (or feeling of passing through a *tunnel*), a sensation of *rising* (or one of *falling*), often followed by a "*click*" in the *head*.*	7. Crookall (1961); (a) "*blackout*", pp. 3, 13, 55, 57, 83, 92, 96, 117, 123, 126, 167; (b) "*tunnel*", ibid., pp. 8, 11, 13, 68, 82, 89, 114, 119; (c) *rising*, ibid., pp. 48, 54, 57, 58, 59, 61, 68, 69, 71, 104; (d) *falling*, ibid., pp. 61, 68; (e) "*click*", Fox, p. 56; Muldoon (1937), pp. 70, 158, 161, 162.
8. "Doubles" leave chiefly via *the head*.	8. Crookall (1961), pp. 16, 25, 36, 42, 58, 62, 67, 83, etc.
9. "*Dual consciousness*" (awareness of two bodies, the "double" and the physical body) and two environments that correspond to them. (If the "double" contains much of the vehicle of vitality, the "world" contacted will be either earth or "Hades"; if it is Astral Body only, the "world" will be "Paradise"). Discarnate souls seen in the former case may be "hinderers", in the latter "helpers".	9. Crookall (1961), pp. 16, 25, 36, 42, 58, 62, 83, 107, 128, 161.

Details given by "Communicators", 1909–15, published in 1916 (J.A.S.P.R.) as to how Astral Projections may be Produced	Corroborative Details given in Testimonies of Astral Projectors (unaware of the "Communications")
10. A rapid ejection (or re-entry) tends to forgetfulness of the out-of-the-body experience of the "double" (e.g. in accidents or with drugs).	10. Crookall (1961), pp. 41, 77, 83, 98.
11. The early course of the "double" is often spiral.*	11. Crookall (1961), pp. 21, 62, 66, 128, 139.
12. "Double" and physical body are united, so long as life lasts, by a luminous extension, "the silver cord" of Ecclesiastes (xii, 6).*	12. Crookall (1961), pp. 5, 6, 8, 11, 15, 18, 20, 25, 27, 29, 30, 31, 33, 36, 43, 44, 47, 50, 56, 57, 61, 62, 66, 71, 73, etc.
13. At death "the silver cord" is composite (consisting of material from (a) the vehicle of vitality and (b) the Astral Body).*	13. Observations made at deathbeds by A. J. Davis in U.S.A. and Stainton Moses in Britain.
14. The "cord" is essentially an extension of the physical and Astral Bodies.*	14. Crookall (1961), pp. 47, 86, 134.
15. The "cord" must be elastic if the released Astral Body is to travel great distances.*	15. Crookall (1961), pp. 20, 43.
16. The newly-released "double" often lies horizontal, just above the body.*	16. Crookall (1961), pp. 18, 26, 27, 28, 35, 44, 46, 48, 51, 60, 71, 75, 76, 82, 89, 92, 98, 102, 103, 104, 182.
17. The independent descriptions of how astral projectors see discarnate souls ("spirits") are identical.	17. Crookall (1961), p. 162.
18. Forward-moving "doubles" leave "a trail of light" behind them.*	18. Muldoon (1929), pp. 13, 93; Yram, p. 62.
19. Cosmic vitality is absorbed and condensed by released "doubles".	19. Muldoon (1929), pp. 23, 30, 31, 35, 68, 84, 82, 90–2; Crookall (1961), pp. 28, 45, 67.
20. Just as the release of a "double" causes a "blackout", etc. (No. 7 above), so its re-entry into the body causes a "blackout", etc.*	20. Crookall (1961): (a) "blackout", pp. 4, 5, 22, 39, 41, 54, 98, 115, 120, 131; (b) "tunnel", pp. 53, 122.

TABLE I—Comparison of "Communications" as to how Astral Projections may be produced (published 1916) with the testimonies of Astral Projectors (given in Analyses published in the writer's The Study and Practice of Astral Projection, Aquarian Press, 1961).

* As regards these thirteen details (Nos. 2, 3, 5–8, 11, 13–16, 18, 20), the "communicators" exhibited greater knowledge of astral projection than any of the scientific experts or any of the esoteric writers on the subject.

Items No. 12, 15, 17, 18 and 20 particularly are inexplicable on the hypothesis that these "doubles" were mental images: they are readily understood on the hypothesis that they were objective.

APPENDIX II

THE CONTRAST BETWEEN *NATURAL* AND *ENFORCED* RELEASES OF "DOUBLES"

		(A) *Natural Releases of "Doubles"*	(B) *Enforced Releases "Doubles"*
PERMANENT RELEASES OF "DOUBLES"	BODY	Soul Body (a) is complete (since none of its substance forms part of "the silver cord"-extension) and (b) is unenshrouded by any of the substance of the vehicle of vitality (since it was all shed at "the second death" about three days after physical death). It can operate fully in its own environment.	As below.[1]
	WORLD	"Highest"—"a glorified earth", i.e., the Soul World or "Paradise"—part of the total earth.	As below.[2]
	CONSCIOUS-NESS	"Highest" — "super-normal" (with telepathy, clairvoyance, etc.) after a "sleep" that averages three days.	As below;[3] no defi "sleep".
TEMPORARY RELEASES OF "DOUBLES"	BODY	Soul Body (a) is incomplete (since part of its material is included in the "silver cord"-extension) and (b) is usually slightly enshrouded by a tincture of the substance of the vehicle of vitality. Glimpses of, but not full entry into, "Paradise" conditions are possible. Release is retarded by crossing hands and feet.	Soul Body (a) is incomp (since part of its materi included in the "si cord"-extension) and (b more or less definitely shrouded by a defi amount of the subst of the vehicle of vit which was forced out of physical body. Release affected by crossing ha and feet.
	WORLD	Either earth or "Paradise" (glimpses only), or both.	[2] Relatively "low" envi ment is contacted: e and/or a semi-dream w (= "Hades").
	CONSCIOUS-NESS	(b) Many see discarnate helpers and their own "silver cord"-extensions. (a) "Highest" consciousness ("super-normal" — with telepathy, clairvoyance, foreknowledge).	(b) Very few see carnate helpers or their "silver cord"-extension (a) Relatively "low" l of consciousness ("s normal"—often with dre and fantasies).

TABLE II. Differences observed when "Doubles" are formed under *Different Circumstances*, i.e., when their release was (a) *Natural* or (b) *Enforced*. These differences are readily explicable on the hypothesis that the "Doubles" were *Objective, Non-physical Bodies* but difficult to explain on the hypothesis that they were merely Mental Images (of Physical bodies). Read upwards.

For details, see R. Crookall, *The Study and Practice of Astral Projection*, Aquarian Press, 1961.

N.B. A "double" (replica) of the physical body may consist of [1] substance from the vehicle of vitality only (in which case it is *simple* in nature), or [2] the Soul Body only (ditto), or [3] the Soul Body plus the vehicle of vitality (part, if the person is incarnate, all, if discarnate), in which case it is *composite* in nature.

APPENDIX III

COMPARABLE "COMMUNICATIONS"

MANY "communicators" other than Mrs Keeler's, cited by Hall in 1916, have given similar, though less detailed, facts regarding astral projection. Whereas the identity of Mrs Keeler's "communicators" could not, in the nature of things, be verified, in some at least of these cases it is more or less well-established. P. E. Cornillier (op. cit., 1921) was offered methods of attaining astral projection in France in 1913 by "Vettillini", a supposed discarnate *Italian*: unfortunately he had "no ambition" in that direction. It would have been interesting, had he accepted and recorded the proffered methods, to compare them with those of Mrs Keeler's "communicators", who were mostly *orientals*.

Some of Mrs Keeler's "communicators" provided further (and highly reasonable) statements. For instance, on p. 40 we noted two important purposes that are served in astral projection (a) the receipt of teachings, advice and help from advanced discarnate souls and (b) the possibilities afforded in projection of helping sick mortals, the dying and the "earthbound", i.e., "co-operation"). These "communicators" mentioned three other purposes.

(a) "Heslop" (*Speaking Across the Border-line*, Charles Taylor, 1912) said that astral projection is a preparation for the "next life", that the frequent "visits" made to the "next world" made things *"familiar"* when projectors come to die; they experience no sudden change and therefore no shock. "A.B." (*One Step Higher*, The C. W. Daniel Co. Ltd., 1937) said the same thing and used the same word, *"familiar"*. Lilian Walbrook's "communicator" (*The Case of Lester Coltman*, Hutchinson, 1924, p. xiv) said, "things seemed *familiar*". A "communicator" of Lord Dowding (*Lychgate*, Rider, p. 35) stated "The place was *familiar*, yet not familiar."

(b) Although an astral projector is in physical embodiment and certain of his loved ones are not, he "visits" them during projections and (though rarely remembering details and, if remembering them, often thinking that the experience was only a dream) he keeps in touch with them. This is important if a child has "passed on", since (we are told) children develop in "the next world". Constance Wiley (*A Star of Hope*, The C. W. Daniel Co. Ltd., 1938) was informed, "The child is taken to meet his parents in their sleep-state, when their spirits have left their bodies." On the other hand, Geraldine Cummins (*Travellers in Eternity*, Psychic Press) was told that incarnate boys will meet their discarnate mother—"they will remember her words and advice and believe it to be their own thoughts". Mrs Keeler's "communicators" (1916, p. 683) stated that these "meetings" do not take place in the normal "next world", i.e., in full "Paradise", but in "a place where one of two who have loved on earth waits for the other to come so they can continue to progress together". Other "communicators" made this point. For instance, that of H. Dennis Bradley (*Towards the Stars*, T .Werner Laurie, 1924) stated: "You must not imagine the place in which they meet is the same as the sphere in which the discarnate souls live-on. It is ... a between-place, as it were, where the atmosphere is not impossible for either the dead or the living." The "communicator" of *I Awoke* (David Stott, 1895, p. 116, Appendix, p. iii) said, "We do not really enter the next state until we leave the psychic world behind us for ever. Our psychic bodies are no more suited to live there than your bodies are for this world ... You cannot pass to us, nor we to you, but in very exceptional and partial ways." This "between-place", which is not full "Paradise" (the normal "next world" of decent folk), is evidently also entered during the process of "communicating"—see Diagram No. 5, p. 209 of the writer's *The Supreme Adventure*, James Clarke, 1961.

(c) These things are possible only because, on the one hand, the loved ones who have "passed on" renounce, for a time, their advancement. "F. W. H. Myers", communicating (Sir Oliver Lodge, *The Survival of Man*, Methuen, 1909, pp. 292, 302), observed that his "missionary spirit" kept him "from felicity awhile". In these below full "Paradise" conditions, discarnate souls are less vital, alive and alert than they would normally be, while on the other hand the (more or less spiritually evolved and therefore astrally-projecting) mortal is, at the time, more vital, alive and alert than in his normal (physically-embodied) condition. The "communicator" of "A.L.E.H." said (*Fragments from*

my Messages) that consciousness was "far more intense", that of
"A.B." (op. cit.) said "most active", and that of Wilfred Brandon
(*Open the Door!*, Alfred Knopff, 1935) used the same words.

Hall (x, 1916, p. 641) made the general observation that Mrs
Keeler's "communicators" had provided teachings as to "the cosmic order" which did not differ from the teachings of the Theo-,
sophists, etc. The idea of man as a microcosm (with a physical
body, including the *vehicle of vitality*, an *Astral or Soul Body* and a
Spiritual or Divine Body), while the universe—"the earth and other
planets"—is a macrocosm with a similar construction (p. 642),
each "star" having "a ruling spirit of its own" (p. 704), has been
given in all esoteric literature from the earliest times and continues
to be given. It has, of course, been replaced by the modern scientific approach. Nevertheless, Dr J. Parton Milum considers that
"The ancient idea that man is a microcosm, or little world in
himself, developing in response to the Macrocosm, or Universe,
and having its counterpart in his own being, is a far more adequate conception than the prevailing attempt to envisage man as
an evolving original." The fact is that there is something to be
said for both conceptions—see *The Supreme Adventure*, p. xxx.

With regard to *the vehicle of vitality*, W. Whately Smith (later
Carington), in *A Theory of the Mechanism of Survival*, the Fourth
Dimension and its Implications (Kegan Paul, Trench Trubner &
Co., Ltd., 1920, p. 162), suggested that, in addition to the physical
or three-dimensional body, we have "a four-dimensional body"
[= the Astral or Soul Body] and that what the Theosophists call
"*the etheric double*" [= the vehicle of vitality] represents "the connecting-link between the three- and four-dimensional vehicles".
This has often been described by clairvoyants, e.g., by the Hindus
(who called it Prânamâyakosha = vehicle of vitality), by Frau
Hauffe in Germany (who called it "the nerve spirit" in *Die Seherin
von Provorst*, 1829, .p. 118), by Dr Rudolf Steiner.(who called it
"*the life body*" and "*the body of* formative forces" in *Theosophy*, etc.,
1910), by Max Heindel (who called it "*the vital body*" in *The Rosicrucian Cosmo-Conception*, 1911), by Phoebe Payne and Dr L. J.
Bendit (who called it "*the etheric body*" in *The Psychic Sense*, Faber,
1943 and *Man Incarnate*, T.P.S., 1957), etc.

The *vehicle of vitality* was also described by many astral projectors, including Vincent Turvy (*The Beginnings of Seership*, Stead's

Publishing House, 1909, pp. 43, 45, 55, 57, 192), Oliver Fox (*Astral Projection*, Rider, pp. 36, 78, 97, 142), Sylvan J. Muldoon (*The Projection of the Astral Body*, Rider, 1929), and Yram (*Practical Astral Projection*, Rider). It was also mentioned by Reine in hypnotic trance (P. E. Cornillier, *The Survival of the Soul*, Kegan Paul, Trench Trubner & Co. Ltd., 1921, p. 191), when she spoke of "the organic part of the fluidic body", said it was "reddish" (whereas the Astral or fluidic body is "blue"), and that it is shed some time after physical death, when (p. 150) it "returns to *terrestrial* matter".

Innumerable "communicators" (in addition to those of Mrs Keeler) describe this important bodily feature and they call its shedding (on an average some three days after physical death) "the second death"—this applies to the following British "communicators": M. Hoey (*I Awoke*, Hoey, 1907, p. 52), A. L. E. H. (*Fragments from my Messages*, Women's Printing Society, 1929, p. 17), of Marjorie Livingston (*The New Nuctemeron*, Rider, 1930, pp. 53–4), of Geraldine Cummins (*The Road to Immortality* and *Beyond Human Personality*, Ivor Nicholson & Watson Ltd., 1932, p. 35), of W. T. Stead (*Communication with the Next World*, Cricket Press, 1937), of Mrs Alice Gilbert (*Philip in Two Worlds*, Andrew Dakers Ltd., 1948 and *Philip in the Spheres*, Aquarian Press, 1952), of Jane Sherwood (*The Psychic Bridge* and *The Country Beyond*, Rider), of Oswald Murray (*The Process of Man's Becoming* and *The Spiritual Universe*, Duckworth, 1921, 1924), of Lord Dowding (*Lychgate*, Rider, 1945 and *The Dark Star*, Museum Press, 1951), of the Revd. Wm. Stainton Moses (*More Spirit Teachings*, Fowler, 1911, p. 77) and of the Revd. C. Drayton Thomas (*Life Beyond Death with Evidence*, Collins, 1928, p. 78).

In America the "communicators" of Mrs Cora L. V. Tappan (*Discourses*, Burns, 1875), of Mrs S. L. Ford (*Interwoven*, Boston, 1905, pp. 25, 160), of Mrs May Wright Sewall (*Neither Dead nor Sleeping*, Watkins, 1921, pp. 293, 301), of H. A. and F. H. Curtiss (*Realms of the Living Dead*, 1917, pp. 57, 58), while in Germany the "communicator" of Fr. J. Greber (*Communication with the Spirit World*, Felsberg, 1932) also described it. Although various terms were used in these "communications", including "*the nerve soul*", "*the principle of life*", "*the unifying body*", "*the double*", "*the astral double*", "*the husk*", "*the after-image*", "*the health aura*", "*the psychic form"*, *"the magnetic vitality"*, *"the magnetic aura"*, etc., they obviously refer to the same important bodily feature as Mrs Keeler's "communicators".

Clairvoyants, astral projectors and "communicators" (other than those of Mrs Keeler) also describe Astral [Soul] and Spiritual [= Divine or Celestial] Bodies and correlate them with corresponding environments ("Paradise" and the true "Heavens" of the Scriptures respectively). In brief, the Keeler "communications", as Hall observed, are essentially identical with innumerable others.

The idea of the absorption of cosmic vitality (the "Prâna" of the Hindus) by the released Astral Body is also given by numerous "communicators" other than those of Mrs Keeler. Anthony Borgia's (*ABC of Life*, Feature Books Ltd., 1945, pp. 36, 109, 111) said, "When you sleep, while your spirit body is absent, your physical body is replenished with the energy that keeps you alive and active. Your body is, as it were, charged with force ..." The "communicator" of *I Awoke* (p. 9) stated: "Life is one; it is an electrical, non-material stream of influences from the great source of life." That of "Quaestor Vitae" (Oswald Murray—*The Process of Man's Becoming*, Duckworth, 1921, p. 147–8) said, "Everyone is a recipient of vitality by influx ... The influx of vitality-containing thoughts is inbreathed through the medium of your atmosphere." "F. W. H. Myers" communicating through Geraldine Cummins (*The Road to Immortality*, Ivor Nicholson & Watson, 1935, p. 68) said, "During sleep this body [= the one that 'acts as an intermediary between the intellect and the physical shape', i.e., between the Astral or Soul Body and the physical body, namely, the vehicle of vitality] ... feeds the physical shape with life-units, with nervous force". "Vettellini" told P. E. Cornillier (op. cit., p. 386) that sleep enables the Astral Body to gather "the vital force" from "magnetic and cosmic currents". He pointed out that "The amount supplied by ... food, respiration, etc., would not suffice to sustain life if the breath of the vital, cosmic force did not come to fortify it. This applies to all living creatures [plants and animals, as well as human beings]."

The idea that discarnate souls can see the gradually increasing luminosity of the Astral Body as it separates from its physical counterpart, given by Mrs Keeler's "communicators" in relation to astral projection, i.e., to *temporary* releases—and it should be noted that "spirits" commonly call mediums "*lights*"—is given by other "communicators" in relation to the act of dying, i.e., to *permanent* releases. "A.B." (*One Step Higher*, The C. W. Daniel Co., 1937, p. 90) was told, "Guardians or guides will be there [at the deathbed]. The actual process of death, the passing out [of the Astral Body] into new conditions sets *a series of vibrations* into action which form a contact with the near relations of the dying man. Those who are in spiritual vibration with that soul will know of his 'passing' and seek him out." "Judge Hatch" (Elsa Barker, *Letters from a Living Dead Man*, Rider, 1914, p. 184) stated: "I knew he was about to die—his body became surrounded by *a peculiar light* [the Astral Body]." "J. V. H." (*Death's Door Ajar*, Rider, 1934, p. 100) similarly said, "The lamp of life burns low on your side and bright on ours. Then we see the earth-flame flicker and know it will soon be out."

The fact that "communicators" other than Mrs Keeler's observed that there is a significant difference between *natural* and *enforced* releases of the double was noted on p. 12. The Keeler "communicators" were referring to *temporary* releases, i.e., astral projection, the "Professor" (communicating) to *permanent* ones, i.e., to death (p. 15).

Examples of "communicators" other than Mrs Keeler's were given in the text concerning the "blackout" (or "tunnel effect") when the Astral Body leaves the physical body, concerning "helpers" and "hinderers" and concerning the Astral Body often appearing as a "mist" or "vapour" during the course of its release from the body.

The statement, given in 1916, that quitting the body in astral projection, i.e., *temporarily*, is "an individual process" is matched by "communications" to the effect that quitting the body *permanently* is also an individual process. Thus, the "communicator" of *I Awoke* (1895, pp. 27, 56) said, "No two souls are alike and no two can have exactly the same experience."

There is no need to cite "communications" to support the Keeler statement that severe illness facilitates the *temporary* release of the "double", since most *permanent* releases, i.e., deaths, are due to severe illness. Nevertheless, according to both the Keeler and other "communicators", the *most satisfactory* temporary projections take place in good health! This apparent contradiction is explained by possible differences between the "doubles" that are released *by people who are non-mediumistic* (a) in severe illness and (b) in good health: those which are projected *readily in illness* are *composite* (consisting of some of the vehicle of vitality as well as the Astral Body) but are *not very satisfactory instruments of the soul* (because the former more or less enshrouds the latter, while the person concerned may, or may not, be of a highly moral and spiritual development, so that the Astral Body may, or may not, be organized and available as an instrument of consciousness), but those which are projected readily *in good health* are *simple* (Astral Body only, more or less organized because the person is highly developed in a spiritual sense, and also of value as an instrument of consciousness because not enshrouded by substance from the vehicle of vitality). Two factors are involved, i.e., facility for projection and availability, after projection, as a vehicle of the soul. *Mediumistic people* have loose vehicles of vitality and always tend to extrude part of that along with the Astral Body—but this enveiling feature generally returns, along the "silver cord", to the physical body, so that the originally composite "double" becomes simple (a process that corresponds to "the second death").

The notion of death as involving "crossing a 'river'" (= "Hades" conditions) was given in great detail in "communications" published by F. H. and H. A. Curtiss (*Realms of the Living Dead*, San Francisco, 1917, p. 27). It is quite often mentioned in "communications".

"Vettellini" the "communicator" of P. E. Cornillier (op. cit., 1921, pp. 107, 122, 279, 288, 387), like the Keeler "communicators", insisted that crossing the hands or feet interferes with the release of the Astral Body. But it is interesting to note that this is not a universal rule. It does not, we suggest, apply to normal healthy people (whose vehicle of vitality is tightly knit with the physical body and who release *a simple "double"*, i.e., *the Astral Body only*). The exceptional cases are mediumistic people, with vehicles of vitality that are loosely associated with the physical body—these tend to release part of the vehicle of vitality along with the Astral Body (i.e. a *composite* "double"). In their case the loose vehicle of vitality seems to act as a drag on the escaping Astral Body and if, in addition, the hands or feet are crossed

(allowing the forces in the vehicle of vitality to circulate), the release of the "double" is rendered still more difficult. "The excep-
tion proves [= tests] the rule" [generalization]. This explanation
of the apparent discrepancy between testimonies, deduced by the
present writer, he later found in the "communications" received
through Mrs Keeler (p. 679) where it was said that crossing the
hands or feet "*mixes the nerve-currents and hinders the exit of the
Astral*" [*Body*]. It was not, however, there stated that the effect
obtains only with those who have loose vehicles of vitality, i.e.,
mediumistic people, and we believe this to be the case.

Cornillier's sensitive, Reine (who was ignorant of psychic
matters), was mediumistic. Among the items that caused Cornillier
to believe in the reality of her "helper", "Vettellini" (op cit., 1921,
p. 279), was the fact that on June 6th, 1913, the latter complained
that Reine had failed to give Cornillier "an important injunction":
this was that when she was alone and trying to release her
"double" "she must install herself in such a position that it will
not be possible for her feet to cross each other, nor for her hands
to join together; for this would prevent her Fuidic [= Astral]
Body from disengaging completely ..." On December 1st, 1913,
while Reine's "double" was released, Cornillier saw her clasp her
hands tensely. Then she unlocked them and expostulated to her
"deliverer": "But they're not crossed, I tell you! What a bother
you are!"

Many who have been through the "Third Degree", in which
one is "raised from the dead", ceremonially involving the temporary release of the "double" as in the ancient Mysteries, will
have wondered why the "double" could not be released (= the
candidate "raised") *until the feet were uncrossed*.

"Communicators" other than Mrs Keeler's (e.g., "Vettellini",
op. cit., 1921, pp. 40, 43, 138, 312, etc., and "Imperator", *More
Spirit Teachings*, Fowler, p. 76) advise little or no food before a
seance, while alcohol (and sometimes tobacco) are forbidden.
They also agree that moral and spiritual advancement is reflected
in the tenuousness (and therefore the projectability) of the Astral
Body. "Heslop" (*Speaking Across the Border-line*, Taylor) said this.
Others use significantly similar terms: the "communicator" of
A. L. E. H. (op. cit.) said that consciousness becomes "far more
intense", that of Wilfred Brandon (op. cit., 1935) "active", that of

Kate Wingfield (*More Guidance from Beyond*, Philip Allan & Co., 1925) "very active", etc. The "communicator" of E. W. Fitzsimons (*Opening the Psychic Door*, Hutchinson, 1933) said it quite specifically: "Advanced souls, who have been in the habit of leaving the body during sleep, require no help at death." "Claude" (Mrs Kelway Bamber, *Claude's Book*, Psychic Book Club) told his mother, "When your body sleeps, your soul comes over here and we spend hours together ... *To do this, people must be spiritually evolved to a degree ...*"

With regard to the idea that the "Paradise" environment, the normal "next world", is related to the "fourth dimension" (so that the Astral Body has also been called the "fourth-dimensional body"), we have already cited two "communicators" other than Mrs Keeler's in this matter. We may also note that the "communicator" of *I Awoke* (David Stott, 1895) gave, in an Appendix, "communications" that preceded those of Mrs Keeler, since they were received in 1891. They include the following remarks: "There *is* a fourth dimension ... The fourth dimension, only guessed at by you, is our first." He went on to speak in a manner very like that employed in the "communications" under consideration (received 1909–11 and published 1916) and the exercises recommended therein: "I think a symbol to be added to the line [one dimension], the square [two] and the cube [three] might be this—a hollow sphere with other hollow and smaller spheres enclosed within it, something like the balls cut by the Chinese. These spheres must be thought of as composed of a kind of elastic fluid; the larger spheres by compression passable through the smaller and the smaller by expansion passable through the larger. *Thus each each sphere can be within or without the others* ... Your world and ours are not like two globes side by side and independent of each other, but *as a Spirit [in the Astral Body] inhabits a [physical] body, so our world inhabits yours* ... Let us call the fourth dimension inter-progression, then the fifth might be called trans-progression."

The "communicators' " statement, given through Mrs Keeler, that a very rapid ejection of the Astral Body (in the case of *temporary* releases) tends to lower the "level" of consciousness and cause forgetfulness of the out-of-the-body experience, is paralleled in cases of *permanent* releases, i.e., death. This is shown in the writer's *The Supreme Adventure* (James Clarke & Co. Ltd., 1961, pp. 21, 30, 37, 46) where various "communicators" are quoted as saying, "Those who die *suddenly* are sometimes even unaware that the change has taken place", "they are in great confusion as to what has happened", "they don't believe they have passed on", etc.

Mrs Keeler's "communicators" stated that, in *temporary* releases of the Astral Body, the latter, often leaves the physical body chiefly via *the head*. Other "communicators", for example, "Heslop" (op. cit.), stated, "The process begins at the feet and emerges from *the head*."

If the newly-released "double" *temporarily* leaves a *horizontal* body it often at first takes up a *horizontal* position not far above the body. Other "communicators" describe this remarkable position as obtaining in *permanent* releases. In Great Britain "Robertson", describing his own "passing" (F. T. Robertson, *Celestial Voices*, H. H. Greaves) stated: "I came to consciousness with my new body resting *parallel over* my old one and about a yard above it ... Then ... I began to take an upright position." "Heslop" said that the newly-born " 'double' generally floats *horizontally* above the body ..." In South Africa, Fitzsimons (op. cit., 1933, p. 19) was told, "It floats *horizontally* over the physical body ..." (Uprighting begins as soon as the "silver cord"–extension is severed.)

We have already pointed out that various phrases used indicate that the "silver cord" is essentially *an extension*: just as Mrs Piper's released Astral Body *"came in"* on her "silver cord" and Crabbe's friend *"came down"* it, so in Germany Greber's "communicator" stated that the Astral Body finds its way back to the body *"along"* it, and in England "Heslop", communicating, said that it returns *"through"* the cord. (Neither Greber nor Heslop had read anything about these matters.) Many "communications" (other than Mrs Keeler's) about the "silver cord" were cited in the writer's book *The Supreme Adventure* (James Clarke & Co. Ltd., 1961, pp. 18, 20, 62, 66, 120, 126, 129, 130, 188).

Mrs Keeler's "communicators" (1916, p. 646) stated that "Even when [the Astral Body is] outside [the physical body] the connection with the physical tends to influence it somewhat." Other "communicators" make this statement. For example, the "communicator" of J. S. M. Ward (*Gone West*, Rider) said that some mortals whose Astral Bodies are temporarily released "wander along the fringe, as it were, [= 'the between-place' of Bradley, p. 59] of the spirit plane [= 'Paradise'] as if their connection with their bodies rendered them only partly conscious of the Astral World in which they moved". The supposed deceased father of the Revd. C. Drayton Thomas, communicating, said the same.

Mrs Keeler's "communicators" stated that, in *temporary* releases of the *Astral Body* the "cord" must be elastic if one is to travel far from the body. This is highly significant in relation to what is said, by other "communicators", to occur in *permanent* releases of the "double" (which here is *composite*, consisting of the whole of the vehicle of vitality as well as the Astral Body). Both the "double" and its extension, the "cord", are here composite and, since it includes substance from the vehicle of vitality, in the early stage of death the "cord" is far from being elastic so that, even with spiritually-advanced people, the "double" is held within quite a short distance above the corpse: the following are examples of distances "communicated"—"*a yard*", "*three feet*", "*a short distance*", "*a little*", "*just over*" and "*near*". After a short time, the "cord" snaps and the "double" uprights. After a further period (about three days) the vehicle of vitality is shed (= "the second death") so that the "double" becomes *simple* (Astral Body only) and its "cord"–extension had indefinite elasticity—the "spirit" is free!

"Communications", other than those that were transmitted by Mrs Keeler, concerning "dual consciousness" were given in *The Supreme Adventure*, pp. 20, 100, 101, 137, 142, 178. Examples of "communications" that refer to discarnate "hinderers" and "helpers" were given in the text above.

The Keeler "communications" (X, 1916, pp. 683, 692) to the effect that one who leaves the body *temporarily* can assure himself of the fact by the sight of his physical body is paralleled, according to other "communicators", in *permanent* releases where a man who has died in his sleep, and therefore without being aware of the fact, is made to realize it by seeing his own corpse. "Philip" (*Philip in Two Worlds*, by Mrs Alice Gilbert, 1948, p. 89) said, "I looked, and it was my body. I looked at myself and saw my own body ['double'] seeming quite real and solid ... I knew I was killed." "Coltman" (Alice Walbrook, *The Case of Lester Coltman*, Hutchinson, 1924, p. 5) stated, "I found those around me could not see me and went back and saw my body, lying dead."

The Keeler "communicators' " description of how discarnate souls appear to mortals who are *temporarily* out of the body, i.e., to astral projectors, as, at least at first, "spirit lights", "tongues of flame", etc. are exactly paralleled in other "communications"—those of Stainton Moses and of Wilfred Brandon were cited in the text above.

The idea given by Mrs Keeler's "communicators" that we mortals are creative is given by many other "communicators". That of J. S. M. Ward (*Gone West*, Rider) described conditions in "Hades" (the environment that corresponds to the vehicle of vitality) and said, "To many spirits, who know no brighter place, this seems full of colours ... This is a land of change, a half-way house [= "the between-place" of Bradley, p. 59], as it were, between the physical and the spiritual [here = 'Paradise'] plane, therefore it seems somewhat unreal and changing *to denizens of either plane* [= *to mortals or to discarnate souls in 'Paradise'*]. So, too, the elements which form it are ever changing, and, being very malleable [= ideoplastic] often assume forms in consonance with the wills of those who pass through them, even when they are sleepers dreaming ..."

"Communicators" other than Mrs Keeler's also stress the importance of faith. That of *Spiritual Reconstruction* (Watkins, 1918, p. 120) advised: "Act as if the thought-world really exists ... This is faith in perfection. See your homes simple, pure and beautiful. See in your neighbour and his affairs order and beauty and be blind to all else. This is bringing the image-making faculty into outer existence. Never mind the failings ... See in all you meet the ideal people of your thought. Have only the single eye."

It will be evident that, although, so far as we are aware, no "communicators" provided so many techniques for the production of astral projection as did Mrs Keeler's, they did provide many identical ideas and the whole philosophy of all these "communications"—some of whom pre-dated Mrs Keeler's—is identical. It is easy to suggest that this fact has no objective implication but it is not possible to prove it. Those who would take this attitude are invited to pay particular attention, in *giving detailed and specific reasons*, to items nos. 12, 15, 17, 18 and 20 of the Table that forms our Appendix I. "He that *gives reason* for what he saith has done what is fit to be done and the most that can be done. He that *gives no reason* speaks nothing, though he saith never so much."

APPENDIX IV

OBSERVATIONS MADE AT DEATHBEDS

NUMEROUS people have made observations at deathbeds that are identical with the statements of Mrs Keeler's "communicators", considered above. This essential identity of content seems inexplicable on the hypothesis that the Keeler "communications" came from supposed "sub-conscious" fragments of the medium's mind: in the first place, the observations that are cited below were made entirely independent of mediumship and therefore of supposed "sub-conscious" fragments of a medium's mind; in the second place, these observations are concerned with death and not with excursions of the Astral Body that were always temporary and often made in a state of *good health*. These (non-mediumistic) observations and the (mediumistic) "communications" have two things in common—the identity of their descriptions and the fact that they describe one process, that of quitting the physical body.

The Keeler "communicators" described the Astral Body as often escaping in *temporary* releases from the physical body from all pores, as leaving chiefly via *the head*, as appearing *like steam* to an onlooker, as "*drawing together*" and "*gradually becoming fully organized*". Identical descriptions are given concerning *permanent* releases by non-mediums. A number of these pre-date the Keeler "communications".

In Great Britain Mrs Annie Brittain (*'Twixt Earth and Heaven*, Rider, p. 65) observed "*a violet mist*" leave a dying body, "*deepening round the head*". It drew together and gradually became defined until it formed "an exact replica of the old body". Mrs G. Vivian, B.A. (*Love Conquers Death*, L. S. Publications Ltd., pp. 117, 153), who observed the "passing" of her mother, saw "*a mist*" which "*gradually took shape*" until it resembled her mother. Mrs Gladys Osborn Leonard (*The Last Crossing*, Psychic Book Club, 1937, p. 196) also reported seeing "*a mist*" leave a dying body. Florence Marryat (*The Spirit World*, F. V. White, 1894), who described the transition of a friend, said, "A film like *a cloud of smoke* gathered above her *head; it acquired the shape of the girl's body.*"

Major W. T. Pole (*Private Dowding*, Watkins, 1919, p. 101) observed "a *shadowy* form above the body". T. E. Morgan (*in litt.*) saw "what seemed like *smoke*", Mrs Alexander (*in litt.*)[1] "a *mist-like* form" which "seemed to be herself", Mrs "Joy" "a black *cloud*", etc.

In America, a literary woman (*Borderland*, III, 1896, p. 271) was present at the death of a baby. She stated: "A grey *mist* emanated from around the *head*. It rose and gradually resolved itself into *the child's similitude* ..." Dr R. B. Hout (*Light*, LV, 1935, p. 209) described the death of his aunt, prefacing his description by the declaration that he had never read anything like it. First he saw "a hazy, *fog-like substance* about two feet above the bed". He continued, "Gradually definite outlines presented themselves; the *fog-like substance* soon ... *resembled the physical body of my aunt*." The mother of Mrs Gwynne Dresser Mack (*in litt.*) saw "a thin *spiral* of white *mist*" rise from her dying husband's body. Mrs Eileen J. Garrett, a clairvoyant who is now a world-famed investigator, who saw her girl die (*My Life as a Search for the Meaning of Mediumship*, Rider & Co. Ltd., 1939, pp. 26, 52, 90), said, "I saw, rising above Ann's body, *a curly, shadowy, grey substance*. When I entered the room it was already gathering itself ... into a *spiral* shape which finally disappeared ..." Mrs Garrett observed the same phenomenon when her son died. When a child, she had seen something like this at the death of birds, etc.—"*a smoke-like substance rising in spiral form* ..." [This was doubtless the vehicle of vitality, i.e., a *simple* "double"]. Later Mrs Garrett (*Awareness*, Creative Age Press Inc., 1954, p. 181) described a *composite* "double" which she saw when a Chinaman died: "I perceived *two small clouds* emitted from his body, one from ... the level of the spleen [= vehicle of vitality], the other from the top of his head [= Astral Body]".

In Australia a friend of Mrs E. Herrick (*in litt.*) saw her father-in-law die. "A sort of *mist* rose from the top of his *head*. It gradually became a replica of the man ..."

Mrs Keeler's "communicators" stated that in *temporary* releases, the newly-born Astral Body often lies *horizontal* not far above the (horizontal) physical body. Observers of *permanent* releases describe the same noteworthy position. They include Major Pole

---

[1] These letters will be deposited with the S.P.R., 1 Adam and Eve Mews, London, W.8.

(op. cit.—*"a horizontal position"*), T. E. Morgan (*"horizontal"*), etc.
Mrs Alice Mortley told Dr W. W. Hall (*Observed Illuminates*, The
C. W. Daniel Co. Ltd., 1926, p. 163) that she had been present at
five "passings": in each case she "distinctly saw, lying *horizontally*
over the corpse, a luminous form which was *recognizable as the
individual*".

Mrs Keeler's "communicators" stated that the course of the
escaping "double" is often *spiral*: a similar description is cited
above.

An important feature of astral projection, mentioned specifically by Mrs Keeler's "communicators" but unrealized by the experts, Drs Lancelin and Carrington (as Muldoon was obliged to
point out), is the existence of the "silver cord". This feature is
said in the "communications" to transmit vitality from the released Astral Body to the vacated physical body, so that its severance ("loosing" to use the word employed by Ecclesiastes xii, 6,
some thousands of years ago) necessarily involves the death of the
physical body. Its many features are readily explained on the
hypothesis that it is a temporary *objective* extension between the
objective Astral and physical bodies, but are quite inexplicable on
the alternative hypothesis that it, and the Astral Body, are mere
mental images.

Florence Marryat (op. cit.) observed: "When she lay back unconscious, the spirit [= 'double'] above, which was still bound to
her brain, heart and vitals by *cords of light like electricity*, became, as
it were, a living soul. The Spirits of her father and grandmother ...
ruptured ... the cords ... Rising between them, she vanished."

Major Pole (op. cit.) observed that "the shadowy form" which
lay "in a *horizontal* position" some two feet above the dying body,
was "attached to the physical body by *two transparent cords*". He
stated, "One of them seems to be attached to the solar plexus
[= the 'cord', or extension, of the vehicle of vitality] and the
other to the brain [= that of the Astral Body] ... Two figures·
stoop down over the bed and seem to break off the 'cords' ... Immediately the 'double' rises ...'"

The Revd. G. Maurice and Irene H. Elliott (*Angels Seen Today*,
Elliott, 1919, p. 123), who saw a woman die, observed: "A *silvern
cord* was attached to the physical and the Soul [= Astral] Body
and the helpers severed this."

Dr R. B. Hout (op. cit.) testified to seeing "*a silver-like substance that was streaming from the head of the physical body to the head of the spirit-double*". He stated: "*This 'cord' seemed alive with vibrant energy* ... At last the connecting strand snapped and the spirit-body was free. The spirit-body, which had been *supine* [= *horizontal*] before, now rose and stood vertically."

The following case, told by Mr "G", was published in *Journ. S.P.R.*, xii, 1908, p. 368. "My wife died at 11.45 p.m. At 6.45 ... I saw, floating through the doorway, three separate and distinct *clouds* in strata ... Slowly these clouds approached the bed until they completely enveloped it. Then ... I beheld, standing at the head of my wife, a woman's figure like a sheen of brightest gold. The figure ... seemed to express a welcome ... Two figures in white knelt by my wife's side, apparently leaning towards her ... Above my wife, and connected with *a cord proceeding from her forehead*, there floated, in a *horizontal* position, a nude, white figure, apparently her Astral Body. With her last breath, as her Soul left the body, the 'cord' was severed suddenly and the 'Astral' figure vanished." (Dr Burgess, an expert in nervous and mental diseases, who was present at this deathbed, wrote: "From my own observations, I can most positively put aside a temporary state of hallucinatory insanity during the time of the vision just recorded ... I knew Mr 'G' well. I had occasion to know that he had never read anything in the occult line.")

Numerous similar cases will be cited in a forthcoming book by the present writer to be called *Events on the Threshold of the After-life.*

These significant events are accompanied by a number of experiences, such as "dual consciousness", mentioned by Mrs Keeler's "communicators". These, which will be considered in a forthcoming book entitled *Experiences on the Threshold of the After-life*, also are corroborated from sources that are entirely independent of mediumship. Daisy Dryden, aged ten, when dying, declared, "I have a new spiritual body ... I can see you all and I can see them ['dead' friends] there at the same time" (J.A.S.P.R., XX, No. 6). Dr Charles Richet, Professor of Physiology at the Faculty of Medicine, Paris, a foremost psychical researcher and one who, in trying to avoid accepting the theory of survival, advanced that of cryptesthesia [= ESP], admitted that cases such as this (involving a young child who could have heard or read nothing about such matters) were most readily explained on the survival hypothesis (*Thirty Years of Psychical Reasearch*, Wm. Collins, 1923). His theory, though ingenious, was unable to deal with certain facts of experience. "Human *experience*," declared Dr Samuel Johnson, "which is constantly contradicting *theory*, is the great test of truth." The astral projectors and observers at deathbeds, cited above as corroborating Mrs Keeler's "communicators", may make the same claim as did the apostles (John iii, 11)—"We speak of what we know, and testify to what we have seen."

APPENDIX V

THE PURPOSE AND OBJECT OF LIFE

ACCORDING to Mrs Keeler's "communicators", "The object of life is to find out what the object of life is." So far as this is regarded as an individual matter, it can be determined by the individual noting what proportion of his "spare time" is spent in what activities. But we are here concerned with this as a general and not an individual question: what is the purpose of earth-life in general? If the conclusions reached above are accepted, we have some information on this head also.

In Germany, Johann Wolfgang Goethe (1749–1832), no doubt rightly, held that the object of life cannot be known completely by mortals—"Man is not born to *solve* the problem of existence", he said, "but to *attempt to* solve it." A Pharisee (St Paul, I. Cor. xiii, 9) similarly maintained, "Our knowledge and our prophecy alike are partial and the partial vanishes when wholeness comes." In Greece, Plato (b. 427 B.C.) long ago considered that the events of this world are imperfect and changing reflections of events in the perfect world of reality. Rousseau (1812–67) lamented the fact that the subject concerning which man was most ignorant was himself. Professor G. Elliott Smith, speaking for the anthropologists in 1927, admitted that this was still true. In the following year another anthropologist, Sir Arthur Keith, declared, "Mind, spirit and soul are the manifestations of the living brain, just as the flame is the manifest spirit of a burning candle." He concluded, "At the moment of extinction, both flame and spirit cease to have separate existence."

Keith's analogy was unwarranted. It was, in fact, on a level with that of untutored savages. When sailors first landed on the South Sea Islands, the natives, who had never seen iron, were fascinated by nails and their uses. The sailors presented them with a number of the coveted objects, whereupon they planted them in the ground with a view to increasing their supply.

The analogy that the eminent Sir Arthur Keith drew between a living man and a wax candle was no less false, and therefore no less misleading, than that which the South Sea Islanders drew between a living seed and an iron nail.

Psychical research was unknown in the time of Goethe and Rousseau and was disregarded by Elliott Smith and Arthur Keith. It has made us independent of mere analogies, which, in this connexion, can never be close and can therefore never constitute valid bases of argument.

Dr Eugène Osty, the Director of the Institut Métapsychic Internationale, Pariš, in his great work, *Supernormal Faculties in Man* (Methuen, 1923, transl. Stanley de Brath), after reviewing the evidence for the existence of telepathy, clairvoyance, etc., pointed out that, if all the various kinds of supernormal cognition were exercised by a single person, "their possessor would excite the stupified amazement of other men". He continued, "Yet such a being, superhuman to our ideas, is a logical possibility." We are now possessed of information that enables us, in considering the object of life, to base some conclusions on established facts.

We may use an analogy so far as procedure is concerned. Suppose we were confronted with a machine that was swathed in tarpaulins. How would we decide its purpose? Having removed the coverings, we would note its components—wheels, levers, gears, etc., and their connections and draw our deductions from the observed facts.

Now psychical science has, to a considerable extent, "taken the tarpaulin" off man, revealing his "components" (faculties such as telepathy, clairvoyance, and foreknowledge, abilities such as astral projection and experiences such as those designated mystical or cosmic), and their "connections" (in the various "selves", namely, the lesser, outer or temporary self which uses the physical body, the psychic self or "Soul" which uses the Soul or Astral Body and the Greater, Inner or Eternal Self, the Over-soul, which uses the Spiritual Body).

First Object—Individualization and Self-consciousness

The Eternal Self is given (apparent) separateness when it assumes, first the Astral Body and then the physical body: in this way personality is formed, with the possibility of responsibility and therefore of moral advance. Many "communicators" say this—

e.g., "Universal Spirit has an individuality through its association with the soul and the body." Again, "Man takes his life from God but he is, in embryo, a Cosmic consciousness which becomes individualised only through incarnation into various states of matter, including your own flesh." "Spirit is part of God's consciousness dwelling within you and animating you. It is not *your* Spirit, but *God's* Spirit in you. The Soul is developed by the combination of Spirit and body." "The soul is the child of the Spirit and body. For the purpose of creating individual man, a part of God, Spirit, allies itself with a physical body. Universal Spirit is non-personal." "A detached part of this Universal Spirit, attaching itself to a new physical body, gradually becomes personal through contact with conditions which you call 'life'."

These "communicators" (? sub-conscious products of fragments of ordinary minds) agree with the ideas advanced by the well-known philosopher, the late Dr C. E. M. Joad in the last book that he published, namely, *The Recovery of Belief* (Faber, 1952, p. 201). "*Spirit ... is timeless*. Its true home is not in this but in another order of reality. [Compare St Paul, Heb. xiii, 14—'Here we have no permanent home but are seekers after the city which is to come'.] In fulfilment of a purpose, it is incarnated in a [physical] body or, perhaps, in a number of successive [physical] bodies [re-incarnation] and so intruded in the time-order ... *mind is brought into being in consequence of the contact of the Spirit with the natural, temporal order, which results from its incorporation in a physical body* ... Since *a mind* comes into existence as a by-product of the soul's incarnation in matter, *its existence is temporary only*. Moreover, it is not in the mind that the unity of the person resides ... *the unity of the person resides, in fact, in a region [The Greater or Eternal Self, the Atman of the Hindus] which is normally inaccessible to consciousness*."

This final and considered judgement of C. E. M. Joad is, of course, identical with the "communications" that we have cited —and the "communicators" said it first; moreover, while various philosophers differ on this matter, "communicators" do not— they are unanimous.

Edward Carpenter (*The Drama of Love and Death*, George Allen & Unwin, 1924, p. 244) took the matter further, indicating the rôle that is played by the physical body in these circumstances. He pointed out: "Limitation and hindrance are a part of the cosmic scheme in the creation of souls. Soul-stuff is capable of infinitely swifter and more extended perceptions than we are usually aware. What purpose does this limitation serve? It subserves the evolution of *self-consciousness* and *the sense of identity*. It was only by pinning sensitiveness down to a point in space and time, by means of a body, and limiting its perceptions by means of the bodily end-organs of sight, hearing, taste, etc., that these new values could be added to creation—the *self-conscious self* and *the sense of identity*. Through the development of identity mankind must ultimately rise to a height of glory otherwise unimaginable."

Dr William Wilson (*After Life*, Rider, p. 192) said, "The purpose of our seeming separateness is that each may realize for himself the God [Greater, Inner, Eternal Self] within and learn that the [lesser, outer, temporary] self must be conquered. Only thus may each become a worthy partaker of the Life of the Spirit when the physical envelope dissolves at death."

The "communicator" of Oswald Murray (*The Spiritual Universe*, Duckworth, 1924, p. 38) said the same as Dr Wilson, before him, and in a wider context—"Our circuit of becoming includes our descent [the 'fall' into matter] as germic [= Eternal] Selves from the central ['Heaven'] state into this outer, physical world, passing through intermediate states [the Soul World or 'Paradise'] before we get here. Becoming endowed with an organism, through human parentage, our *self-consciousness* unfolds, and we re-ascend [= the resurrection out of matter] on our return circuit self-consciously, through the same states but in inverse order, from the circumference to the centre, through which we descended. *We descended as units of conscious life, but we re-ascend as self-conscious finite selves.*"

We suggest that individualization and self-consciousness, due to assumption of a physical body (communicated from "the other side" and held by eminent philosophers, medical men, etc.) is the first object of earth-life.

SECOND OBJECT—REALIZATION OF INTER-DEPENDENCE

The second recognized object of life is complementary to the first. In spite of the formation and development (through the partial incarnation of Greater Selves in physical bodies) of a number of lesser selves, or personalities, mankind needs to remember the essential unity of all selves, the fact that *we are all "members one of another"* (Ephes. iv, 25).

Greater Selves are "branches of the true Vine" (John xv, 1), of God-in-manifestation. This object, therefore, consists in the practical expression of man's fundamental nature in the course of daily life.

The following are examples of such "communications". "Man's being is not, as you fancy, some atom by itself: all are parts of 'one stupendous whole'." "One great purpose in the earth-life is the revelation of God. Love means giving, thinking outside oneself. Love is a stream that flows outward all the time."

Again, "The love we feel for one another is intangible to those on earth. But here love lives and is a tangible thing. Without love you are spiritually dead. With love you are a partner of the Divine Creator Himself."

THIRD OBJECT—EXPRESSION OF THE ETERNAL SELF THROUGH THE TEMPORARY SELF

The third object embraces the first two. The selves that we know (and the self that we show to others) are lesser selves, mere temporary fragments, or partial incarnations, of Greater and Eternal Selves, of Over-souls.

One of the objects of earth-life is the expression and manifestation of the Greater Self through the lesser self—particularly by way of bodily acts; in the language of the Bible, the Kingdom of God is thus brought down to earth.

So long as this object remains imperfectly attained, St Paul's complaint applies to us all: "What I would, that I do not; but what I hate, that I do" (Rom. vii, 15). Thus from our point of view (seeing only in part), there seems to be opposition between the lesser self, or personality, and the Greater Self, or Individuality, between the "old Adam" and "Christ in you".

It is only when the corn of wheat falls to the ground and dies that it brings forth fruit (John xii, 24). Real selfhood is attained only in the surrender of the lesser self: "Thy will, not mine, be done" (Luke xxii, 42).

This is not an arbitrary invention of theologians, it is implicit in the nature of man and of God.

"The proper meaning of orthodoxy," wrote Dr W. R. Matthews, "is simply true, or right, opinion. In practical affairs everyone recognizes the value of having true opinions.

"Life itself is a practical affair and we are unlikely to make much of it if we have false opinions concerning the world, our nature and our relations with God."

Fourth Object—Character Formation

The fourth object is the acquisition of experience and of self-control, the formation of character. According to psychic "communications", this process incidentally organizes the psychical and spiritual bodies, rendering them efficient instruments of the Greater Self after bodily death.

There are innumerable warnings that, although earth-life may seem hard, since the acquisition of certain virtues is facilitated while in the physical body, people who neglect this opportunity will long to come back to earth-life; they will find the after-life infinitely harder than earth-life. Here are examples of such communications.

"Do not wait until you come over here. Set to work at once. Gain control of self. Then empty yourself of self."

Again, "Earth is the school for the spirit. The lessons of patience, calmness and forgiveness must be learned either in earth-life or in the after-life. What you call trifles are often the really important lessons. ..."

Fifth Object—Desirable Habits

The fifth object of life is the formation of desirable mental habits. These are necessarily carried forward into the after-life and this object is a special aspect of the previous one.

Once again, the physical body can be either a help or a hindrance; its relative sluggishness tends to fix habits, good or bad.

Hence, as Jesus indicated in the parable of the Talents (Matt. xxv, 14), earth-life tends to be a seed-time and the early after-life a harvest-time. The forces which we ourselves infused here into our word and deeds must inevitably work themselves out in the hereafter.

The above is an advance on orthodoxy, since, not only is the teaching given but the rationale of the process also is indicated. Here is a "com-munication" to this effect.

"What are your most valued possessions? Love, health, time, etc.? Decide which they are and observe how you are guarding them. Beware what you really desire.

"The free choice is yours, only choose, do not muddle along until, unconsciously, you have fashioned habits which are your paste jewels. The time will come when you must abide, for a while, by your choice.

"Earth-life is more selective than the after-life—a greater chance to waste yourselves, a greater chance to develop. You are on earth to find out what things are worth doing and what are not. Do not wait until you pass on; it would be so much harder later."

Sixth Object—Balance

The sixth object is all-round, or balanced, development, the wholeness which was the ideal of the Greeks: nothing too much, and nothing neglected.

The physical, intellectual, psychical, aesthetic and spiritual aspects of man's total nature all call for due attention and development, yet none must be over-emphasized.

The control of the emotions is an important element in this general purpose. Since the physical body retards and dulls the emotions during earth-life, when, at death, it is shed, emotions of an uncontrolled and painful nature—self-pity, fear, depression, anger, resentment, etc.—tend to run wild and to be more intractable and distressing than before.

The temporary possession of a physical body affords a unique opportunity of attaining balanced developments and, in particular, of keeping the emotions within due bounds. From this it will be clear that, so far from being avoided, suffering is immeasurably intensified and prolonged by the expedient of suicide.

The teachings briefly outlined above were obtained by the writer by the analysis of numerous psychic "communications". Their value is independent of their origin: "Note what is said, not who says it."

They agree, in the main, with the orthodox teachings of religion and psychology, but go further. Moreover, they inhere in an eminently reasonable scheme concerning the nature of man (both here and hereafter) and of God—a scheme and philosophy which receives considerable support from psychical science.

They emphasize the value of deliberately expressing desirable thoughts and emotions through the physical body in specific acts and words (and of avoiding the expression of undesirable thoughts by those means).

Otherwise great opportunities are missed in attaining the objects for which we came into the world (Prov. iii, 27). He who, by words and deed, benefits his neighbour incidentally organizes and vitalizes his own Spiritual and Psychical bodies, the instrument, or vehicles, of the spirit and soul respectively.

When he enters the after-life these bodies will be in a condition at once so efficient and so beautiful that they were compared by Jesus to "a wedding garment" (Matt. xxii, 11).

SEVENTH OBJECT—CREATION

As Mrs Keeler's "communicators" (and many others) said—and as most people discover for themselves sooner or later in their lives—we are *creative*: to a certain extent we (eventually) modify our bodies, create our environments and attract our friends. Our object here must clearly be to "create" that condition of body, that environment and those friends we really want, to do so deliberately and definitely (not vaguely and unconsciously to "create" those we do not really want, those that will not bring lasting satisfaction because they are contrary to our true nature). Life, to a large extent, with its partial successes and partial failures, is finding out whether we really wanted, or did not want, certain things. We "create" them and then test them against the satisfaction they bring us. Oscar Wilde said, *"Any man can become a successful business-man, if he gives his mind to it—that is his punishment!"* Amido (*The Wisdom of the Spirit*, Amica, 1943, p. 12) *warned: "Take heed what ye pray [= yearn] for—ye shall surely get it!" You will, indeed, tend to create and attract it. Experience, it has been said, is the best school—but the fees are high.*

EIGHTH OBJECT—INTEGRATION, SALVATION

Although the soul's survival of bodily death is universal and automatic, its attainment of immortality, of eternal life, is conditional,

as was held by Mrs Keeler's "communicators" (X, 1916, p. 653)
The lesser self must be integrated with the Eternal Self if it is to
achieve immortality: in the words of St Paul (I Cor. xv, 44), "The
perishable being must be clothed with the imperishable and what
is mortal must be clothed with immortality."

> Build thee more stately mansions, O my soul,
> As the swift seasons roll!
> Leave thy low-vaulted past!
> Let each new temple, nobler than the last
> Shut thee from heaven with dome more vast,
> Till thou at length are free,
> Leaving thy outworn shell by life's unresting sea!
>   OLIVER WENDELL HOLMES (*The Chambered Nautilus*).

ACKNOWLEDGEMENTS

For permission to make brief extracts from copyright material, the writer tenders grateful thanks to the publishers and authors listed below. Special acknowledgement is made to the American Society for Psychical Research for permission to quote from their *Journal* (Vol. X, 1916, pp. 632–60; 679–708; Vol. XII, 1918, pp. 39–60) and to Laura A. Dale, the Editor of the *Journal*, for her kind replies to his various enquiries. Those who are interested in astral projection owe much more to the publishing house of Rider & Co. Ltd. than to all the others put together: we are indebted to them for such works as *The Projection of the Astral Body* by Sylvan J. Muldoon and Hereward Carrington (1929), *The Phenomena of Astral Projection* (1951) by the same authors, *Practical Astral Projection* by Yram, *Astral Projection* by Oliver Fox, *The Mystery of the Human Double* by the Hon. Ralph Shirley, *Psychic Certainties* and *Man Outside Himself* both by Prevost Battersby, *My Occult Case Book* by Frank Lind, *Man's Unknown Journey* by Staveley Bulford, etc., representing pilot studies for the subsequent work of Professor Hornell Hart, Director of the International Project for Research on E.S.P. Projection (*Proc.* S.P.R., 50, 1956) and others. Thanks are due from the writer to *Psychic News* for permission to reprint (in Appendix V) part of an article by him which was printed in that Journal in Dec. 1955.

Alcuin Press: Stanley Bedford, *Death—An Interesting Journey*, pp. 53, 114.
Alfred A. Knopf: Wilfred Brandon, *Open the Door*, 1936, p. 24.
American S.P.R.: X, 1916, pp. 632–60; 679–708; XII, 1918, pp. 39–60.
Andrew Dakers Ltd.: Alice Gilbert, *Philip in Two Worlds*, 1948, p. 89.
Aquarian Press: R. Crookall, *The Study and Practice of Astral Projection*, 1961, pp. 8, 11, 13, 68, 82, 114, 119, 140.
Aries Press Inc.: Sylvan J. Muldoon, *The Case for Astral Projection*, 1936, p. 24.
Borderland, III, 1896, p. 271.
C. W. Daniel Co. Ltd.: "A.B.", *One Step Higher*, 1937, p. 90; Constance Wiley, *A Star of Hope*, 1938; Dr W. W. Hall, *Observed Illuminates*, 1926, p. 163.
Charles Taylor: F. Heslop, *Speaking Across the Border Line*, 1912.
Creative Age Press Inc.: Mrs Eileen J. Garrett, *Telepathy*, 1941, pp. 40, 51, 59–60, 103, 104, 128–9, 192; *Awareness*, 1943, pp. 17, 45, 90, 92, 116, 135–6, 138.
David Stott: Anon., *I Awoke*, 1895, pp. 27, 56, 116.

Duckworth & Co. Ltd.: Oswald Murray, *The Process of Man's Becoming*, 1921, p. 147; *The Spiritual Universe*, 1924, p. 38.

Faber & Faber Ltd.: Phoebe Payne, *Man's Latent Powers*, 1938, p. 51; Dr J. H. M. Whiteman, *The Mystical Life*, 1961, p. 62; C. E. M. Joad, *The Recovery of Belief*, 1952, p. 201.

F. W. White: Florence Marryat, *The Spirit World*, 1894.

Fate Magazine: 1961, p. 85.

Feature Books Ltd.: Anthony Borgia, *ABC of Life*, 1945, pp. 36, 109, 111.

Felsberg: Fr. J. Greber, *Communication with the Spirit World*, 1932, p. 111.

Fowler, L. N., *More Spirit Teachings*, p. 76.

Garrett Publications Inc.: Mrs Eileen J. Garrett, *Adventures in the Supernormal*, 1949, pp. 7, 143, 164, 165–6.

George Allen & Unwin Ltd.: Edward Carpenter, *The Drama of Love and Death*, 1924, p. 204.

Hamish Hamilton Ltd.: Dr Gardner Murphy, *The Challenge of Psychical Research*, 1962, p. 159.

Harrap: Dr Horatio Dresser, *The Open Vision*, p. 40; Arthur Ford, *Nothing So Strange*, 1958, p. 21.

Hutchinson Ltd.: F. W. Fitzsimons, *Opening the Psychic Door*, 1933; Lilian Walbrook, *The Case of Lester Coltman*, 1924, p. 5.

Harper's: Professor Ian Stevenson, M.D., July, 1959.

Ivor Nicholson & Watson Ltd.: Geraldine Cummins, *The Road to Immortality*, 1932, p. 68; *Beyond Human Personality*, 1935, p. 98.

James Clarke & Co. Ltd.: R. Crookall, *The Supreme Adventure*, 1961, pp. 53, 54, 131.

John Murray: Mary E. Monteith, *The Fringe of Immortality*, 1920, p. 40.

Kegan Paul, Trench Trubner & Co. Ltd.: Dr H. Carrington, *Modern Psychical Phenomena*, 1919, pp. 146–54; *Higher Physical Phenomena*, 1920, p. 266; W. Whately Smith, *A Theory of the Mechanism of Survival*, 1921, pp. 3, 45, 48, 88, 95, 107, 114, 195, 386, 462; Alta Piper, *The Life and Work of Mrs Piper*, p. 115.

L.S. Publications Ltd.: Mrs G. Vivian, B.A., *Love Conquers Death*, pp. 117, 153.

La Revue Métapsychique, 1932.

Light: LV, 1935, pp. 209, 249; LXXVII, 1957, p. 53; LXXX, 1960, p. 59.

London Forum: March, 1935.

Moore, J. C.: Dr J. Kerner, *The Seeress of Prevost* (trans. Catherine Crowe), 1845.

Methuen Ltd.: Dr E. Osty, *Supernormal Faculties in Man*, 1933; Sir Oliver Lodge, *The Survival of Man*, 1909, pp. 292, 302.

Parapsychological Monographs, No. 2, 1960; No. 3, 1961.

Philip Allan & Co. Ltd.: Kate Wingfield, *More Guidance from Beyond*, 1925.

Psychic Book Club: Mrs Kelway Bamber, *Claude's Book*, Mrs Gladys Osborn Leonard, *The Last Crossing*, 1937, p. 196. .

Psychic News: 2 February, 1963.

Psychic Press Ltd.: Geraldine Cummins, *Travellers in Eternity*.

Rider & Co. Ltd.: Muldoon, S. J. & Hereward Carrington, *The Projection of the Astral Body*, 1929, pp. xvii, xxv, 89, 101–2, 167, 212, 237; Elsa Barker, *Letters from a Living Dead Man*, 1914, p. 184; "J.V.H.", *Death's Door-Ajar*, 1934, pp. 78, 100; Ralph Shirley, *The Mystery of the Human Double*, p. 119; J. S. M. Ward, *Gone West*, 1917; Marjorie Livingston, *The New Nuctemeron*, 1930, p. 36; Sydney T. Klein, *The Way of Attainment*, 1924, p. 85; Countess Nora Wydenbruck, *The Paranormal*, 1939, p. 150; Annie Brittain, *'Twixt Earth and Heaven*, p. 65; Mrs Eileen J. Garrett, *My Life as a Search for the Meaning of Mediumship*, 1939, pp. 5, 26, 52, 90; Dr William Wilson, *After Life*, pp. 82, 192; Yram, *Practical Astral Projection*, p. 99; Judge Dahl, *We are Here!*, p. 145; Staveley Bulford, *Man's Unknown Journey*, 1941, p. 133.

Routledge & Kegan Paul: Richard Wilhelm, *The Golden Flower*, 1931.

S.P.R.: *Journ.* VIII, p. 311; LXIII, p. 368; XLI, p. 240.

T. Fisher Unwin Ltd.: Professor C. Flammarion, *Death and its Mystery*, III, 1923, p. 113.

T. Werner Laurie Ltd.: H. Dennis Bradley, *Towards the Stars*, 1924.

Watkins: *Spiritual Reconstruction*, 1918, p. 120; Major W. T. Pole, *Private Dowding*, 1919, p. 101.

Women's Printing Society: "A.L.E.H.", *Fragments from My Messages*, 1929, p. 17.

Wright & Brown Ltd.: W. T. Stead, *Life Eternal*, 1933, p. 79.

Other recommended books:

PRACTICAL TECHNIQUES OF ASTRAL PROJECTION

Dr Douglas Baker. *Illustrated.* In astral projection consciousness vacates the physical body and temporarily inhabits an astral (emotional) body which possesses its own organs of sensation! Author—who has experienced "many thousands of astral projections"—describes five stages of this phenomenon and explains the necessary routines for projecting to each stage in turn through relaxation, visualization and breathing techniques. In addition to providing historic examples of astral projection (including astral manifestations in the House of Commons), Dr Baker relates some of his own experiences while travelling on the astral plane.

THE THEORY AND PRACTICE OF ASTRAL PROJECTION

EXPLORATION IN A WORLD BEYOND THE BODY

Anthony Martin. Introductory guide to out-of-the-body experiences, replete with fascinating case histories, and presenting detailed techniques for releasing the astral body. Author presents compelling evidence for the possibility of leaving the physical body in a second body, while retaining full consciousness and feeling. *Includes:* Occult anatomy; The silver cord; The double in history; Preliminary exercises for releasing the double; Constitution of the astral body; Nature of the double; Visualization exercises; Spontaneous projection.

ASTRAL DOORWAYS

J. H. Brennan. *Illustrated.* The Astral Plane denotes a realm of visual imagination where thoughts become pictures which are more 'real' than dreams. This absorbing book provides four main 'Doorways' through which one may enter the Astral Plane, namely, the five Tattva symbols; The Tarot; The Qabalah; the Oriental Hexagrams of I Ching. Before these are attempted the reader is asked to practise concentration and visualization exercises, which must be perfected before a successful astral journey can be made. Author cites a novice who had completed his first Path Working and commented: 'I feel marvellous. That was a most therapeutic experience.'

YOUR PSYCHIC POWERS

AND HOW TO DEVELOP THEM

Hereward Carrington Ph.D. The *only* detailed instruction manual of its kind for developing trance-mediumship! This amazing book, written by a dedicated psychical researcher, was based on notes he wrote for circulation amongst members of New York psychical societies. Introduces the whole range of psychic manifestations, including the human aura, telepathy, clairvoyance, crystal gazing, automatic writing, obsession and insanity, hypnotism and mesmerism, astral projection, spirit- and thought-photography and materialization. Guidance is also given in distinguishing between true and false phenomema. Dr Carrington maintained: **'. . . we are all more or less mediumistic or psychic, and need only to cultivate our powers in order to develop them, and bring them to maturity.'**